**PRESENTED TO**

---

**BY**

---

**DATE**

---

**OCCASION**

---

**AUTOGRAPH**

---

*You will seek me and find Me, when you search for Me
With all your heart. (Jeremiah 20:13)*

# HEAVEN'S DOORWAY

## Meditations: For Ministers Of Reconciliation

Rose Margaret Lataillade-Beane, Ph.D.

Copyright © 2014 by BLD & Associates, LLC
Cover and door illustrations by Jehanne Lataillade

"Scripture quotations marked (AMP) are taken from AMPLIFIED BIBLE Copyright © 1954, 1958, 1962, 1964, 1965, 1987 by The Lockman Foundation. All rights reserved. Used by permission (www.Lockman.org)"

Scripture quotations marked (NKJV) are taken from the New King James Version. Copyright © 1982 by Thomas Nelson, Inc. Used by permission. All rights reserved.

Scripture quotations marked (NIV) are taken from the HOLY BIBLE, NEW INTERNATIONAL VERSION®, Copyright © 1973, 1978, 1984 by International Bible Society, Used by permission of Zondervan. All rights reserved.

Scripture quotations marked (NLT) are taken from the Holy Bible, New Living Translation, copyright © 1996. Used by permission of Tyndale House Publishers, Inc., Wheaton, Illinois 60189. All rights reserved

All pictures of doors were obtained from photos online and by permission as appropriate during 2014-15; refer to the reference page for specific sources.

The Sheep fold illustration for the Door of Life is "Copyright New Tribes Mission, used by permission" (Don Pederson, March 31, 2015 don_pederson@ntm.org).

ISBN: 978-0-692-42753-8-51499-9-780692427538

## Dedication

This book is dedicated to:

*In memory of my parents*, **Guillaume and Edith Lataillade**, my heroes who instilled faith and education as a foundation for living.

My husband, **Joe Beane, Jr.** whose love is unconditional and has always allowed me to excel in my gifts and talents, my heart belongs to him;

My son, **Joseph Lee Beane** who has been my champion and an inspiration and who is a man of gentleness, wisdom and understanding;

My *daughter*-in-law, **Cayla Canelas** and her family for accepting my son into their family;

My sisters: **Nadia & Jehanne**; My brothers: **Adrien, Ronald, Joel**, and *in memory of* **Jocelyn and Patrick**, each of them have help develop who I am.

My name sake and sister-in-law, **Margaret Lataillade** who is a shining light in the way for me.

My very best friend, **Brenda Thomas**, who encouraged me to put my life stories in this devotional and it, has made the difference; she also led me to my Church family.

Last but not least, my surrogate Mother and Aunt, **Adrienne Barnave** who is 94 years of wisdom and understanding at the reading of these Meditations. She is my Mother's sister and has stood in for Mommy since her death in 1993.

To all of my nieces and nephews (*too many to mention*) especially the Dixon Guys: JP - my godchild, David, Tony, Nicky, Gerard; Robert Hagerman, Shamael, Nadia, Kamau, Kashmir, Dominique, Danielle, Richard and all my grand nieces and nephews; all of the wives and partners, too. I love you and pray blessings and the manifold favor and grace of God for your lives.

# Acknowledgments

Special thanks to my **sister, Jehanne**, for her gift and deep love of God –she saw the vision that God gave me for this work and illustrated it so beautifully as the Cross of Christ symbolizing Heaven's Doorway.

Special thanks to my brother, **Claude Ronald**, who led me to the Lord in April 1978, a mighty man of God, coached the fine-tuning of these writings, collaborated to write the addition of the Door Keys to the Meditations and who wrote the first Foreword of this book.

Special thanks to my pastors, **Drs. Ron and Georgette Frierson** who have planted and nurtured me in the Word with their teaching ministry and example and for the foreword offering.

My **New Covenant Christian Center Church Family**.

Special thanks to **Dr. Elsa Olvera** for the editing of this work and has blessed me as a coach and encourager in my life.

Special Thanks to **Dr. Valarie Powell**, my dear friend, who so encouraged me as she was blessed reading through the meditations.

Special thanks to **Ger'Quia Abner's TAGDesigns** team for digitalizing my vision of Heaven's Doorway Cross front and back cover concepts.

# Contents

Acknowledgements
Forewords
Introduction

## Reconciliation to God

1. Door Of Salvation – Revelation 3:20
2. Door Of Life – John 10:7-9
3. Door of Certainty – Revelation 3:7-8
4. Door Of Rest – Revelation 4:1

## Reconciliation of Others

5. Door of Witnessing – Colossians 4:2-3
6. Door a Purpose – 1 Corinthians 16:9
7. Door of Opportunity – 2 Corinthians 2:12-15
8. Door of Faith – Acts 14:27

## Reconciliation of Mind

9. Door Of Influence – Proverbs 26:14
10. Door Of Choice – Genesis 4:6-7
11. Door of Utterance – Psalm 141:2-3
12. Door Of Judgment – James 5:8-9

## Door Keys
## Prayer of Salvation
Afterword
Sources

# First Foreword

When I was about 10 or 11 years old, my family was living on Hazelwood in Detroit Michigan. My younger sister, *Rose* Margaret and I were playing out in front of our house. My parents had given strict instructions to us that Margaret was not to cross the street to play, but to stay on our side of the street. Hazelwood was not a major thoroughfare, but a small side street with not a lot of traffic, only local traffic. Our house was about three or four houses from the corner of the block. I was older and not restricted to playing on the side of the street where we lived. So, I was free to cross the street whenever I wanted to play on the other side.

One day, I was playing on our side of the street with my friend. I thought Margaret was playing in front of the house. While I was playing with my friend on his porch, my sister called out to me from the wrong side of the street. I'm not sure how I responded, but, shortly thereafter, my sister began to cross the street. Suddenly, a car came careening around the corner, the driver we learned later was drunk. The driver braked but was not fast enough. The car hit Margaret and she fell several feet on the wrong side of the street away from where I was playing. I remember thinking, "Oh no, she's not supposed to be on that side of the street, she will get in trouble…" What a thought to have at that moment!

Reconciliation in Greek is *katallage* and it means "exchange." It is used as a term in business to speak of money changers, exchanging equivalent values. In this context, we use the idea of a "fair" exchange. God wants to make a fair exchange with us. The payment for sin is not cheap. It is expensive! We can't make the exchange even if we wanted to because whatever we have, will not balance the scales!

Knowing this, God decided to make us an offer only a fool would refuse! Let's not be that fool!

We did not go seeking God, He came seeking us. We did not bring the deal to God; He brought the deal to us. God had forgiveness in one hand and the payment for it in the other. God said, "I want you to have forgiveness/salvation, but you can't have it unless you pay for it, but you can't pay for it because you don't have what it takes. But, I got a deal for you! I'll give you the necessary payment so you can exchange with me. All you have to do is believe me, take the gift and make the exchange!"

This book of meditations written by my sister, *Rose Margaret*, is a walk of reconciliation. God is in the business of reconciling us to Himself. He did not need us to accomplish His work, but in His wisdom, He ordained that we would be fellow laborers with Him in this Ministry of Reconciliation. In our zeal in this work, let us do it with passion and with love.

My sister has a very unique perspective which incorporates my thoughts and feeling about our Ministry of Reconciliation. The concept of DOORs perfectly identifies our role, our position, and our part in this walk of reconciliation. These Doors show us God's heart in reconciliation from the *Door of Salvation* to the *Door of Rest*. Through every portal, every entry way, every entrance, God is leading us, God is preparing us, God is prompting us, God is encouraging us, God, is molding us to be all that He would have us to be in Christ Jesus.

My thoughts that day long ago were very childish when my sister Rose Margaret was hit by a car. I was a child and I thought as a child. My concern should have been how my sister doing versus on whether we would get in trouble for which side of the street she was on. My friend and me even tried to get her back on the "right" side of the street so she wouldn't get in "more" trouble but she was too weak. *I was focused on the wrong problem.*

In our Ministry of Reconciliation, we can be certain that in reconciling others to God through Christ, we are dealing with the right problem – they are out of fellowship with God – and the right solution – restoration of fellowship through Jesus Christ. God is not concerned about our faults as much as he is concerned about our healing, our restoration, and our place of peace.

Let's learn to see reconciliation through God's eyes.

*Claude Ronald Lataillade*

# Second Foreword

From time to time, we are fortunate to be given the opportunity and honor to read a work of art in the field of Christianity that is not only a good read but also a great study. That is precisely the feeling we have about Dr. Beane's tireless effort put forth in penning what I would term as a study guide in prayer and meditation…called Heaven's Doorway.

This study guide uses *doors* as a symbolic opening to move through and into a more personal relationship with God. This concept helps to make this read a study that develops in you a passion to not only master the door just entered but helps you to seek a hunger and thirst for revelation knowledge. Dr. Beane's work challenges you to seek more and more revelation knowledge from God's Word after entering each *door* and before moving on to the next *door*. As I mentioned before, this book is not just a read but a study in Biblical meditation that is a must have in the library of the serious Bible student who is endeavoring to get closer to and establish fellowship with God.

Matthew's gospel chapter 7:7-8 says, "Ask, and it will be given to you, seek, and you will find, knock, and it will be opened to you." Verse 8 reads, "For everyone who asks receives, and he who seeks finds, and to him who knocks it will be open." Finally, in John Chapter 10, the scripture tells us that Jesus is that Door. *Isn't it* amazing how God uses *doors* to promote growth and development in our relationship and fellowship with Him? This book is vital to your Christian growth because it is designed to reconcile you to God and it helps you to develop intimacy with Him along the way.

You will enjoy the nuggets of truth that have been deposited on the other side of each door. You will discover as we did that this is a treasure that must be a part of your personal library. Each door you open will take you closer to fulfilling your destiny in life to answer the call to greatness! We pray that you will enjoy it as much as we have.

*Blessings*

Drs. Ron and Georgette Frierson

# INTRODUCTION

"Now all things are of God, who has reconciled us to Himself through Jesus Christ, and has given us the ministry of reconciliation."
(2 Corinthians 5:18, NKJV))

In 2008, the Lord gave me twelve (12) scriptures all related to *doors*. I began writing my meditations. It was not until 2014 that I titled my writings, "*Heaven's Doorways*" in a detour I took to write a blog. I decided to use the theme for a blog until the Lord said, "*I didn't tell you to write a blog.*" Later, the Lord from an inner voice told me, "*Heaven only has one door.*" That is how the title, "Heaven's Doorway," emerged. A doorway is an entrance, a door, a front entrance, an entry way, it is a means of achieving or escaping from something [Encarta Dictionary: English (North America)]. Heaven only has one entrance and that doorway is Jesus Christ. ***Jesus is the one door to the truth, the way, and the life.* When we are reconciled to God through believing on the Lord Jesus we accept the mantle for the ministry of reconciliation through Jesus Christ, who is Heaven's Doorway.**

My perspective of Heaven's Doorway borrows from the Fruit of the Spirit to make an analogy. The nine (9) virtues/ graces characterize the Fruit of the Spirit but the Fruit of the Spirit is one and indivisible (Nelson, 2002). Likewise, Heaven's Doorway is characterized by 12 doors of reconciliation but Heaven's Doorway is one and indivisible.

The first four meditations concern our **Reconciliation to God** through Jesus Christ, Heaven's Doorway, through the Door of Salvation, the Door of Life, the Door of Certainty, and the Door of Rest. The second quad deals with the **Reconciliation of Others** to God through the Door of Witnessing, the Door of Purpose, the Door of Opportunity, and the Door of Faith. The third quad describes the **Reconciliation of Mind** through the Door of Influence, the Door of Choice, the Door of Utterance, and the Door of Judgment.

**Reconciliation to God**. The Holy Spirit lays out a path for each of us to follow if we have ears to hear. My heart in its search has always known the journey had the promise of the **Door of Salvation** which beckoned me to the kingdom of God which is righteousness and peace and joy in the Holy Ghost. It is on this path that I have taken where I *made* a choice for salvation and thereby entered the **Door of Life** where a table is set before me where I dined with my Lord and where I am saved and where I go in and out and find pasture. The **Door of Certainty** is when I know my purpose and I have the faith to believe that nothing is impossible because there is a door that *remains open* to work all things together for my good. The **Door of Rest** is the mighty assurance and peace knowing my faith pleases God and that He is a rewarder of those who diligently seek Him and He ask me to come up a little higher in my walk with Him and go in and out of *Heaven's Doorway*.

**Reconciliation of Others.** The second set of writings share my walk as I work out my salvation. The **Door of Witnessing** is my willingness to prepare myself through continual prayer to be ready to share the gospel and not be ashamed to tell my story of what God has done for me. The ***Door of Purpose*** is the wisdom to be still and wait on the Lord for it is His purpose that I serve when an effective door is opened to me, not by my will but His will must be done. The ***Door of Opportunity*** is the awesome anointing of awareness we need for service as a Minister of Reconciliation…if I have the audacity to wait for God's timing, so, when I open my mouth God will fill it as an instrument of His peace and love and the saving light of the world will shine through. The ***Door of Faith*** is but that measure of faith, even the size of a mustard seed, but when I rehearse all that God has done for me and I act on what I believe, this act of faith can move mountains.

***Reconciliation of Mind.*** The third and final set of writings share my experience of the love of God that is exceedingly, abundantly more than I can express in my own words only if they are anointed. The reconciliation of mind comes from renewing the mind with the engrafted Word of God to ensure right believing. My own walk has taken me to the ***Door of Influence*** when the state of my mind was set before me to locate my faith. Although the realities I faced were challenging there is always the doorway that leads to the light of hope. The next meditation is at the precipice at the ***Door of Choice*** whenever I know what the right thing is, but the challenge is either to do what is right or to deny the truth and fall into an abyss of the dark night of the soul separated from the light I seek. Every choice is the gift of free will. The ***Door of Utterance*** is a call to stillness and to live under the restrained power of the Holy Spirit to silence my tongue unless it is to live by every Word that proceeds out of the mouth of God. The ***Door of Judgment*** finds me calling on patience and kindness towards others and withholding judgments to seek the wisdom of reconciliation which is the very peace Jesus gives.

***Door Keys.*** The Door Keys offering goes one step further to provide the scriptural implications that each reader can study as the Holy Spirit leads and to go even deeper sanctifying our temple with the tools that wisdom and revelation provide according to *Proverbs 24:3-4*:

> Through wisdom a house is built,
> And by understanding it is established;
> By knowledge the rooms are filled
> With all precious and pleasant riches.

This set of writings took me through a personal walk of reconciliation and it is my desire that each meditation will equip you and speak to you through your own walk of reconciliation to God, to others, and of mind. As you follow the path the Holy Spirit has laid for you through *Heaven's Doorway, you will find keys in the wellspring of that secret place of silence that opens each inner door of your spirit.*

***Cover Concept.*** Jesus said, "And I, if I be lifted up from the earth, will draw all peoples to Myself" (John 12:32). My desire is that this whole work point to the Lord Jesus Christ, my Savior, my healer, my deliverer! Therefore, the cover concept of the Resurrection Cross symbolizes the finish work Jesus on the cross as Heaven's Doorway. It was created in 1986 by my sister, Jehanne Lataillade and was digitized by TAGDesigns. The cross is draped with the burial cloth symbolizing the resurrected Christ as the Lord of glory, who self-proclaimed that He is Heaven's Doorway. The gold color represents perfection and is the characteristic of King Jesus, our redeemer, reconciler, and mercy seat.

The 12-Meditations in this book can be read once a month for the 12 months of the year; meditating on the reading and digesting it throughout the month and reflecting on the questions at the end of each meditation. Or, the 12-Meditations can be read straight through, one after another, like a novel. Basically, you can decide how you would best like to approach reading these meditations with the central theme being the great commission and leading others to Christ, *Heaven's Doorway*.

# Reconciliation To God

Our reconciliation to God is God-authored, God-driven and God-assuring.

# 1

# DOOR OF *SALVATION*
*Revelation 3:20 (NKJV)*

(Christart, 2015)
*Behold, I stand at the door, and knock.
If anyone hears My voice
and opens the door, I will come in to him,
and will dine with him, and he with me.*

"Behold, I stand at the door and knock, if anyone *hears and listens and heeds* My voice, and opens the door, I will come in to him, and will sup [dine] with him, and he [will dine] with me" (The Foundation Lockman, 1987). There is a knocking at the door of our hearts and it is the Lord who stands at the door and knocks to get our attention and to gain permission to enter. The Lord does not break-in as the devil does. The Lord does not bust in and "crash" the party as it were...but admittedly, He stands at the door knocking, actively, requesting permission to enter. He is waiting for a response. He is waiting for each one of us to answer the knock at the door of our heart. *He waits for us to hear, listen and heed His voice.*

This door opens from within our hearts. It also seems that there is some question as to whether we are receptive to hear the voice of His knocking. First of all, will we hear Him physically with our ears and mentally with our mind? Will we hear His still small voice, spiritually? Are we even paying attention? There are so many distractions occupying our attention these days. Are we plugged in and tuned out with our MP3 player, I Phone, IPAD, Droid, Smartphone, and GPS or to any one of the endless array of attention hijacking technologies? Are we listening on multiple levels amid these strategic distractions [*Texting, Snap Chat, Twitter, Facebook, etc*]?

If we hear on any level, the question then becomes, will we "*heed*" His voice? To heed His voice, the questions becomes, do we know His voice? This is now a choice that each of us must make when we stand on the opening side of the door of our heart. Through the progression of this scaffolding...we find that **if** we 1) hear 2) and listen 3) and heed His voice, and invite Him in; He will come inside and "dine" with us. We find that the dining is a mutual experience because He said, I will come in to you, and will dine with you and you will dine with me [*my translation*]. This signifies that an immediate relationship will be developed and an exchange will take place, "I with him and he with me." Dining is an *experience*. There are perhaps several courses to the meal and *experience* signifies being served. In fact, on several occasions, Jesus has identified this experience as the "*one thing that is needed*" and the "*good part*" in *Luke 10:42*.

Jesus is standing at the door, knocking. You can choose to listen to hear and heed His voice. Hearing is a choice. The glory of His presence, when you open the door and invite Him in… is unspeakable. He will come in through the open door of your heart of hearts to dine with you and you with Him. It is life changing.

In 1978, I was engaged to be married on April 22. I had planned my wedding to the minute with a countdown script beginning 30 minutes before the ceremony, leaving out no detail. Yet, I had not planned on Jesus standing at the door, knocking that day. That day that was the beginning of my eternal life through the person of Jesus Christ. That day, I saw Jesus, who is my salvation, standing at the door of my life knocking. That day Jesus came in and enlarged my territory.

The ceremony took place at the beautiful sanctuary of St. Theresa's Catholic Church in Detroit, Michigan. Having become concerned about my countdown…I wanted to check with the people at the front vestibule of the Church. I was in the catacombs, behind the altar, waiting for the signal to come through the tunnel to avoid the guest seeing me. Well, the perfectionist that I was, I couldn't wait and ended up falling down three steps and breaking the high heel of my right bridal shoes ($60). This was not good because I had prayed for a *perfect* wedding and this would not do. I was alone.

> "Behold, I stand at the Door, and knock…"

There was no cell phone (*in those days*) and no way to communicate with the wedding planner in the front of the Church. In *panic*, I wanted to rush to the department store, where I had purchased the shoes and get a replacement pair before the ceremony began. *Insanity*! Right? Well, God had another plan because Jesus was *already making His way* to knock on the door of my heart that day.

You see, two weeks before my wedding day, my brother Claude Ronald had shared the *Good News* of the Gospel of Grace and led me to the Lord. He shared the simple *Good News* of the Gospel of Salvation that we had experienced as children at St. Agnes Catholic

School, looking at film strips of missionaries spreading the gospel. *The Good News Filmstrips*: Jesus was born, He lived, He died for our sins, and He has risen and is alive that we might have eternal life and forgiveness of sins.

Claude Ronald called me from California to make sure I knew and accepted the Lord Jesus Christ before I was married. Well, after assenting to accept the Lord, I hung-up, and waited for something to happen. Lightening! Anything! Yet, I didn't feel the immediate power of the transformation of my spirit and the salvation of my soul.

God in His infinite wisdom and *sense of humor* waited until my wedding day, Saturday, April 22, 1978 at 2:00 p.m. The risen Lord Jesus Christ, in His fullness, knocked at the door of my heart. Somewhere between walking down the aisle on my father's arm, self-consciously worried about leaving the broken heel of my shoe in the middle of the center aisle, and my shock at Father Morand's sermon declaring my perfectionism… my heart fully opened and totally submitted to the love of Jesus. I surrendered my whole life to Him in that grace saving moment…and the glory of the risen Lord anointed my head with the oil of His mercy and grace… and the fullness of God came  *into* me and *upon* me and *through me.* I experienced from that point on in the ceremony the presence of the Lord…because I was listening and heard Him knocking, I knew His voice, and I answered the door of the *mercy seat of my soul* and of *my recreated spirit* (*heart*). I have *never, ever* been the same and I continue to bask in that same presence, now as I am telling the story of my miraculous salvation and ongoing relationship with the Lord. On my wedding day, I was crucified with Christ, it is no longer I who live, but Christ lives in me; the life that I live in the flesh [*my body*] I live by faith in the Son of God who loved me and gave Himself for me *(Galatians 2:20)* …the truth, the life and *Heaven's Doorway*!

As we work out our salvation, the Lord has also promised according to Matthew 7:8-9 (NKJV) that we can: "Ask and it will be given to you; seek and you will find; knock and it will be opened. For everyone who asks receives, and he who seeks finds, and to him who knocks it will be opened." This is the assurance of Salvation.

Jesus is knocking! Open the door of your heart to Jesus! You will, never, ever, be the same. What a glorious time you will share in the presence of the Lord when you experience this miraculous relationship. You will be transformed into the Temple of the Holy Spirit. His tabernacle! His sanctuary! Goodness and mercy will follow you all the days of your life and you will truly dwell in the house of the Lord forever (Psalm 23:6). Jesus is knocking! Let Him come in! He is the truth, the way, and the life (John 14:6) and we are transformed into new creatures (2 Corinthians 5:17). Salvation is a gift from God; accept it and *Enter Heaven's Doorway...*

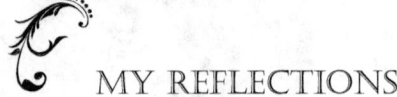

## MY REFLECTIONS

1. Read Revelation 3. Focus on verse 20.

2. What is God saying to you in this passage? About the *Door of Salvation*? _____
   _____

3. What is God saying to you about your reconciliation to God?
   _____
   _____

4. Jesus expects three responses to His knocking; for you: 1) to hear, 2) to listen, and 3) to heed His voice. Have you answered the call of Salvation? Share your experience:
   _____
   _____

**If you have not accepted the call, and you desire to answer the call, go to the Prayer of Salvation in the back of this devotional.**

5. Describe your dining experience with the Lord?

   _____
   _____

6. Describe how your life has changed since you open the Door of Salvation?

   _____
   _____

7. Identify at least one way you can share your salvation experience with others?

   _____
   _____
   _____

## Reconciliation to God

## Door Keys #1

### Door Of *Salvation*
### *Revelation 3:20 (NKJV)*

Behold, I stand at the door, and knock. If anyone hears My voice and opens the door, I will come in to him, and will Dine with him, and he with me.

## *Scriptural Implications:*

1. Why is He at the door?
2. How long has He been standing at the door? How long has He been knocking? How long will He wait?
3. Is He knocking and calling?
4. Why is there an expectation that a meal will be prepared for Him?

## *Key Words:*
*How do these words frame and focus what God is saying to us through this scripture verse?*

- Behold
- Stand
- Knock
- Anyone
- Hears
- My Voice
- Opens the Door
- I will … (come in and Dine)

# 2

## Door of *Life*
John 10:7-9 (NKJV)

(New Tribes Mission, 2015)

*Then said Jesus to them again,
"Assuredly, I say to you, I AM the door of the sheep.
All who ever came before Me are thieves and robbers,
but the sheep did not hear them. I am the door.
If anyone enters by Me, he will be saved,
and will go in and out and find pasture."*

I believe that there is a "doorway to heaven." From cover to cover, the Bible talks about that doorway. Throughout John 10, Jesus declares that He is that doorway to heaven plain and simple. ***"I assure you, most solemnly I tell you, that I Myself am the Door for the sheep"*** (John 10:7, AMP). Jesus also promises that *"if any man enters in (that door), he shall be saved."* This chapter is also a prelude to the crucifixion, in verse 11 Jesus declares, "*I am the Good Shepherd. The good shepherd risks and lays down His [own] life for the sheep*" (John 10:11).

What does Jesus' analogy to a Shepherd and the metaphor of his followers as sheep mean to us today? This is of course a metaphor, an allegory, or a parable to provide an illustration to increase common understandings. In this passage, it explains that Jesus, "said to them again" and that is because having told the story using the illustration the people did not understand what he was talking about. So, Jesus made it plain to them with the analogy of the sheepfold and shepherding. John 10:7, "I am the door of the sheep and if any man (sheep) enters in, he will be saved (Nelson, 2002).

Psalm 23 clearly expands that promise and details the promise of entering Heaven's Doorway for each of us.

In John 6:37, Jesus says, "All that the Father gives Me will come to Me and the one who comes to Me I will by no means cast out." That assurance is repeated in John 10:28, "And I give them eternal life, and they shall never perish; neither shall anyone snatch them out of My Father's hand." When I first got saved, this was what made the revelation, a clear understanding deep in my spirit. I used to go around singing a song by the Clark Sisters, "He's got the whole wide world in His hand!" In the palm of His hand, the Father is holding us very near to care for us watchfully and affectionately (1 Peter 5:7) as we cast our cares on Him (Psalm 55:22). However, we should understand that we must "enter in" by way of Jesus to have that assurance of salvation.

Through the door, we find Jesus is the way, the truth, and the LIFE (John 14:6).

Through the door, we have communion with the Holy Spirit (2 Corinthians 13:14).

Through that door, we dwell in the secret place of the Most High and abide under the shadow of the Almighty, sheltered by the God that is above all gods (Psalm 91:1).

Through the door, I can say that the Lord is my refuge and my fortress and I can trust Him in safety and security (Psalm 91:2).

Through the door, the Lord has set His love upon you and therefore will deliver you and set you on high because you (the sheep) know His name (Psalm 91:14).

Through the door, you can call upon the Lord and He will answer you; He will be with you in trouble, He will deliver you and honor you Psalm 91: 15-16).

Through the door, we find Jesus is the way, the truth and the life (John 14:6).

Through the door, all things are made new (2 Corinthians 5:17).

Through the door, because we are as He is, *we call those things which do not exist as though they are* --- whatever it is it was already done on the cross at Calvary (Roman 4:17)

Through the door, the Lord with long life will satisfy you and show you His salvation (Psalm 91:15-16). Hallelujah!

Through the door, the Lord makes you to lie down in green pastures (a place of rest); He leads you beside still waters; He restores your soul (mind, will, intellect and emotions); He leads you in the paths of righteousness; He anoints your head with oil (Psalm 23).

Through the door goodness and mercy will follow you all the days of your life; and you will dwell in the house of the Lord, forever (Psalm 23:6).

Through the door, by His stripes you are healed and He heals all our diseases (Isaiah 53:5, Psalm 103:3).

Through the door, you will not fear or will you be ashamed, disgraced but you will forget the shame of your youth because all of your sins are forgiven and are in the sea of forgetfulness (Isaiah 54:4).

Through the door, NO weapons formed against you shall prosper and every tongue that raises against you in judgment you can condemn which is your heritage (Isaiah 54:17).

Through the door, no temptation shall overtake you and with every temptation, the Lord will make a way of escape so that you will be able to bear it (1 Corinthians 10:13).

Through the door, you can say to the Mountain be removed and be cast into the sea; it will be done (Matthew 21:21).

Through the door, whatever things you ask in prayer, believing, you will receive them (Matthew 21:22).

Through the door, if you lack wisdom you can ask God for it and He will give it liberally and without reproach (James 1:5).

Through the door, you will receive power when the Holy Spirit comes upon you; you will speak with tongues, rivers of power, love and a sound mind will flow from you (Act 1:8, Acts 2:4, 2 Timothy 1:7).

Through the door, you can call things that do not exist as though they did;

Through the door, the Word of God is very near you it is in your mouth that you might speak it and do it and in your heart that you might believe it (Deuteronomy 30:14; Romans 4:17).

Through the door, you have this confidence in the Lord that if you ask anything according to His will (which is His Word), He hears you; and if you know that He hears you, whatever you ask, you know that you will have the petitions that you ask of Him (1 John 5:14-15).

> "I AM the Door of the sheep…"

Through the door, as He is (Jesus at the right hand of the Father in Heaven), so are you in this world (1 John 4:17).

Through the door, we walk in the Spirit and we do not fulfill the pressures of our bodies, instead, we walk in the Fruit of the Spirit which is love, joy, peace, patience, kindness, goodness, faithfulness, gentleness, and self-control (Galatians 5:16, 22).

Through the door, you are blessed with every spiritual blessing in the heavenly places with Christ (Ephesians 1:3); you have access by one Spirit to the Father (Ephesians 2:18); you are strengthen in the inner man according to God's riches in glory that Christ may dwell in your heart through faith (Ephesians 3:16-17; and God is able to do exceedingly, abundantly, above all you can ask or think according to the power that works in you which is the same power that raise Jesus Christ from the dead (Ephesians 3:20).

So, what shall we say then: if you choose to walk through the Door of Salvation, which is Jesus Christ, the Good Shepherd, God will be for you and greater in you than He that is in the world (1 John 4:4)!

I could go on and on about the promises and evidence that the Bible gives and that Jesus specifically declares in the gospels when He walked on the earth. Yet, His Words in red are very clear for even the most casual observer: ***"I am the door. If anyone enters by Me, he will be saved, and will go in and out and find pasture."*** Jesus went on to tell us the second promise in addition to salvation; He said, **"If anyone enters in by Me, <u>He will…*go in and out and find pasture.*</u>"**

In my opinion, to better understand what it means to "*go in and out and find pasture*" we must spend time with Psalm 23. Psalm 23 says the Lord is my Shepherd, "*He makes me to lie down in green pastures.*" I close my eyes, I see Jesus and He restores my soul. My body is the temple of the Holy Spirit, when I am still, my mind is quieted; my thoughts like a veil are held back freeing my will, intellect, imagination and emotions …I enter in through Jesus, the door. "I am crucified with Christ, but Christ lives in me; and the life I now live in the flesh I live by faith in the Son of God, who loved me and gave Himself for me" (Galatians 2:20). I find that the secret place of pasture is right here –right now--- inside of me in the well of my spirit. I can go in and out and find pasture. Pasture, where I find love, joy and peace that restores my soul and that is how I am able to access the goodness and mercy and the loving-kindness that follows me all the days of my life (Psalm 23:6). The pasture is the kingdom of God inside me where power resides that is righteousness, peace and joy in the Holy Spirit.

Sheep enter the sheepfold through a doorway which is guarded by the Shepherd. The Shepherd lies across the threshold of the doorway throughout the night in vigil to ward off thieves, robbers, or various predators. This sheepfold represents the hedge of protection the Lord has placed around us (Psalm 32:10; Job 1:10)). My heart is the dwelling place of the Holy Spirit; a place of refuge, a fortress from everything external, every circumstance, every situation, every issue and every visible and invisible distraction

(Psalm 91). This is our hiding place, the *tabernacle* and *sanctuary* within us where we can go in and out and find pasture. Jesus lies across the threshold of our soul as a mercy seat. When I speak in my unknown tongue, I transcend all my worries casting all my cares and my petitions, at His feet and I come boldly to the throne of God where I can find mercy (Psalm 32:10). Greater is He that is in me then he that is in the world (1 John 4:4) and He draws me nearer to Him in my stillness. How magnificent that the Most High God created each of us to commune with Him right where we are…to look and seek inside ourselves only to find we are one with Him and we have access. It is in these moments of still communion that our cup overflows.

    1 Corinthians 2:9 (NKJV) says, but as it is written, "Eye has not seen, nor ear heard nor have entered into the heart of man things which God has prepared for those who love Him."

    Come to Jesus. He is the door. If you accept Jesus as your personal Lord and Savior (Shepherd), you have entered in by Him; you will be saved and will go in and out and find pasture through *Heaven's Doorway*.

## MY REFLECTIONS

1. Read the John 10. Focus on verses 7-9.

2. What is God saying to you in this passage? About the *Door of Life*?
   _____
   _____

3. What does it mean to you, to go in and out and find pasture?
   _____
   _____

4. How does Psalm 23 expand the promise of the Door of Life?
   _____
   _____

5. What does it mean to you to have communion with the Holy Spirit (2 Corinthians 13:14)? _____
_____

6. Describe the life that 1Corinthians 2:9 promises to those who love God?
_____
_____

7. What is the life you can declare you have because of 1 John 4:17?
_____
_____
_____

# RECONCILIATION TO GOD
## DOOR KEYS #2

### DOOR OF *LIFE*
### JOHN 10:7-9 (NKJV)

Then said Jesus to them <u>again</u>,
"<u>Assuredly</u>, I say to you, <u>I AM</u> the door of the sheep.
All who ever came before Me are thieves and robbers,
but the sheep did not hear them. <u>I am</u> the door.
If <u>anyone</u> enters by Me, he will be <u>saved</u>,
and will go <u>in and out</u> and find <u>pasture</u>.

## *Scriptural Implications:*

1. Why Did Jesus have to say it "Again"?
2. Why is Jesus so confident? What assurances does it give us?
3. Who are the "sheep"?
4. What are the "thieves and robbers" saying?
5. Are there other ways to get into the sheep hold?

## **Key Words**:
*How do these words frame and focus what God is saying to us through this scripture verse?*

- Again
- Assuredly
- All
- Hear
- I am
- Anyone
- Saved
- In and out
- Find pasture

# 3

## DOOR OF *CERTAINTY*
Revelations 3:7-8 (NKJV)

(ClipArtOf, 2015)

"These things says He that is true,
He who has the key of David,
He that opens and no one shuts,
and shuts and no one opens:
I know your works.
See, I have set before you an open door,
and no one can shut it;
for you have a little strength, have kept My Word,
and have not denied My name."

Revelations 3:7-8, presents an awesome certainty and assurance, an open door that no one can shut! I believe that the door opens at the moment of salvation – *never again to be shut*.

    The open door that no one can shut is entrance to the way, the truth, and the life.
    The open door that no one can shut is Christ standing at the door knocking and you inviting Him into your life as Lord and Savior. [Revelation 3:20]
    The open door that no one can shut is the one that was opened in heaven with a trumpet which beckons you to, "Come hither." [Revelation 4:1]
    The open door that no one can shut is a door of utterance but we must continue in prayer and watch in the same thanksgiving that God would fill our mouths that we may speak the mystery of Christ, the hope of glory. [Colossians 4:2-3]
    The open door that no one can shut is the judge standing before the door beseeching us to not forsake kindness and mercy towards one another lest we be judged. [James 5:9]
    The open door that no one can shut is the door opened unto you to preach the Gospel but to wait on the Spirit and be led by the Spirit who will fill your mouth. [2 Corinthians 2:11-15]
    The open door that no one can shut acknowledges that sin lies at the door and its desire is for you, but you have the power to rule over and master it because no temptation has overtaken you that is not common to man; but God is faithful, who will not allow you to be tempted beyond what you are able, but with the temptation will also make a way of escape, that you may be able to bear it. [Genesis 4:6-7; 1 Corinthians 10:13]
    The open door that no one can shut is that great and effective door that is opened to you for the great commission knowing that there are many adversaries – yet, no weapons formed against you shall prosper and every lying tongue you will condemn because that is the heritage of the servants of the Lord. [1 Corinthians 16:9, Isaiah 54:17]
    The open door that no one can shut is Jesus, the door of the sheep; you know His voice and the promise, if any man enter in, he shall be saved, and shall go in and out, and find pasture. [John 10:7-9]

The open door that no one can shut is the metaphor of the door turning on its hinges, we are called to go expand our sphere of influence to share the love of God and not be lazy and selfish with the word of promise. [Proverbs 26:14]

The open door that no one can shut is the door of our lips that we would ask that God put a guard over the door of our mouth and keep watch over our lips recognizing like Isaiah that we are of unclean lips and we dwell among those with unclean lips except the Lord touch our lips and purge our sin to speak kindness and truth. There is therefore, no condemnation for those who are in Christ Jesus who walk according to the Spirit. [Psalm 141:2-3, Isaiah 6-5-7, Romans 8:1]

The open door that no one can shut is the door of the Lord's mercy, the Lord's great love that we are not consumed for His compassions never fail; they are new every morning; great is the Lord's faithfulness and loving-kindness towards us. [Lamentations 2:22-23]

The open door that no one can shut is Jesus as a human offering for sin, He has borne our grief and carried our sorrows, He was smitten by God and afflicted, He was wounded for our transgressions, He was bruised for our iniquities; the chastisement of our peace was upon Him, and by His stripes we are healed. [Isaiah 53:4-6]

The open door that no one can shut is He that is able to do exceedingly, abundantly above all that we ask or think, according to the power that works in us. [Ephesians 3:20]

The open door that no one can shut is whom the whole family in heaven and earth is named according to the riches of His glory, to be strengthen with might through His Spirit in the inner man, that Christ may dwell in your hearts through faith; that you, being rooted and grounded in love, may be able to comprehend with all the saints what is the width and length and depth and height – to know the love of Christ which passes knowledge; that you may be filled with all the fullness of God. [Ephesians 3:15-19]

The opened door that no one can shut is the Fruit of the Spirit: love, joy, peace, patience, kindness, goodness, faithfulness, gentleness, self-control against such there is no law. [Galatians 5:22-23]

The open door that no one can shut is that God has not given us a spirit of fear, but of rivers of power, and of love and of a sound mind.

The open door that no one can shut is that Love has been perfected among us in this, that we may have boldness in the day of judgment; because as He is, so are we in this world. [1 John 4:17]

The open door that no one can shut is the confidence that we have in Him, that if we ask anything according to His will, He hears us, whatever we ask, we know that we have the petitions that we have asked of Him. [1 John 5: 14-15]

The open door that no one can shut is that I can do all things through Christ who strengthens me. [Philippians 4:13]

The open door that no one can shut is being anxious for nothing, but in everything by prayer and supplication, with thanksgiving, we let our request be made known to God; and the peace of God, which surpasses all understanding, will guard our hearts and minds through Christ Jesus. [Philippians 4:6-7]

The open door that no one can shut means we can meditate on these things: whatever is true, whatever things are noble, whatever things are just, whatever things are pure, whatever things are lovely, whatever things are of good report, if there is any virtue, and if there is anything praiseworthy.

> "See, I have set before you an open Door, and no one can shut it..."

The open door that no one can shut means that we can cast the whole of our care [all your anxieties, all your worries, all your concerns, once and for all] on Him, for He cares for you affectionately and cares for you watchfully. [1 Peter 5:7 AMP]

The open door that no one can shut is not hindered by the cares of the world and the deceitfulness of riches, or the lust of other things; nor that persecution and tribulations will snatch the Word that was sown on stony places, among thorns and that did not take root (Matthew 13:18-23) it awaits the sower to sow the Word on good ground. In this way we will not allow ourselves to become unfruitful but we will meditate the Word and nurture it deep into the wellsprings of our heart where our faith will work because it is rooted and grounded in love. [Matthew 13:18-30]

The open door that no one can shut *stays open* and we can go in and go out and find pasture. We can find that open door in the temple of the Holy Spirit. Our bodies are the temple of the Holy Spirit and we are His tabernacle. We are building that tabernacle as we receive this awesome promise of God and the assurance that God knows our strength. God knows we are weak but that when we are weak He is strong to work on our behalf. God cannot work through our puny efforts but God can work by His Spirit and by His grace.

The open door that no one can shut is He makes us to lie down in green pastures. God desires that we rest and receive the window of heaven blessing that there will not be room enough to receive it. God desires that we rest, give and receive good measure, pressed down, shaken together, and running over will be put in your bosom. [Malachi 3:10, Luke 6:38]

The open door that no one can shut stays open and just as those who enter in and are saved can go in and go out and find pasture, the Lord will come in and dine with you and you will dine with him in the table set before your enemies. [Revelation 3:20]

The open door that no one can shut stays open for goodness and mercy to follow you all the days of your life and you will dwell in the house of the Lord forever! [Psalm 23:6]

The open door that no one can shut stays open so we can enter His gates with thanksgiving and praise and worship Him. "Bless the Lord, O my soul and all that is within me bless His holy name! Bless the Lord, O my soul, and forget not all His benefits; who forgive all your iniquities, who heal all your diseases, who redeem your life from destruction. Who crowns you with loving-kindness and tender mercies, who satisfy your mouth with good things, so that your youth is renewed like the eagles" [Psalm 103:1-5].

The open door that no one can shut stays open that we will dwell in the secret place of the Most High and abide under the shadow of the Almighty, and say of the Lord, "He is my refuge, and my fortress; My God, in Him I will trust." [Psalm 91:1-2]

The open door that no one can shut is because we have set our love upon Him, therefore He will deliver us; He will set us on high, because we have known His name. We can call upon Him, and He will answer us; He will be with us in trouble; He will deliver us and honor us. With long life He will satisfy us, and show us His salvation. [Psalm 91:14-16]

The open door that no one can shut is an awesome promise and assurance of the benefits of being a Christian saved by grace and filled with the Holy Spirit, equipped with the power that raised Jesus from dead and a life after death in eternity with God.

The open door that no one can shut lets me know that nothing can separate me from the love of Christ; we are persuaded that neither death nor life, nor angels, nor principalities nor powers, nor things present nor things to come, nor height nor depth, nor any other created thing, shall be able to separate us from the love of God which is in Christ Jesus our Lord. [Romans 8:37-39]

The door that no one can shut brings every spiritual blessing in this life that are irreversible and cannot be cursed [Numbers 25:1-18].

The open door that no one can shut is my Door of Certainty which is the same yesterday, today and forever ...*Heaven's Doorway*.

## MY REFLECTIONS

1. Read Revelation 3. Focus on verses 7-8.

2. What is God saying to you in this passage? About the *Door of Certainty*?
   _____
   _____

3. What does verse 7-8 mean to you?
   _____
   _____

4. What can you expect from the Door that always remains open?
   _____
   _____

5. Why is it called the Door of Certainty?

   _____
   _____

6. Why would God give us this assurance?

   _____
   _____

7. Explain why the Door of Certainty is a type of Christ Jesus?

   _____
   _____

# Reconciliation to God
## Door Keys #3

### Door Of *Certainty*
### *Revelation 3:7-8 (NKJV)*

"These things says He that is <u>true</u>,
He who has the <u>key of David</u>,
He that <u>opens and no one shuts</u>, and <u>shuts and no one opens</u>;
I know your works. See, I have <u>set before you</u> an <u>open door</u>,
And no one <u>can shut</u> it; for you have a <u>little</u> strength, have <u>kept</u>
My Word, and have <u>not denied</u> My name."

### *Scriptural Implications:*
1. Who is "He"?
2. What are the "Keys of David"?
3. Why couldn't we "open" the door?
4. What are the "works"?
5. Are there other ways to get into the sheep hold? If so, what are the consequences?

### *Key Words*:
*How do these words frame and focus what God is saying to us through this scripture verse?*
- True
- Key of David
- Opens no one can shut
- Shut and no one opens
- Know
- See
- Little
- Kept
- Not Denied

# DOOR OF *REST*
*Revelation 4:1 (NKJV)*

(ClipartOf, 2015)

*"After this I looked, and, Behold, a door was opened in heaven: and the first voice which I heard was as it were of a trumpet speaking with me; saying, 'Come up here, and I will show you things which must take place after this.'"*

In the Revelation 4:1 passage, John, the apostle, was in the Spirit, when he saw "a door standing open in heaven." John was caught up in the Spirit in heaven looking at the door standing open. Another way that this is mentioned in the Bible is "the heavens were opened."

The voice John heard before in *Revelation1:10* said, "I am the Alpha and the Omega, the First and the Last." In *Revelation 19:11*, the voice is called the "Faithful and True." John said, the voice sounded like a mighty trumpet blast. This voice spoke to him.

On March 27 1992, around 1 p.m., my Mother died. When I received the news…my mind and my world spun out of control. I felt like a balloon losing its air, flying and ping ponging in chaos. In the midst of my utter despair, a voice that sounded like a *mighty trumpet blast,* audibly called out my name, twice. "Margaret! Margaret!" I immediately knew it was the voice of my God, my Savior, my Shepherd, my refuge, my fortress, my righteousness, my holiness, my salvation, my sanctification, my Alpha and my Omega, My Redeemer, the one that is faithful and true. In that moment, peace that *passed all understanding* filled my mind and heart in its fullness. I knew in that moment that my Mother was absent in the world and present with the Lord. I knew that I knew that everything would be alright.

> "Behold, a Door was opened in heaven"

I believe that "the heavens were opened" to me. I believe that the Lord was saying, "Come up here and I will show you what must happen in the future." I experienced the presence of the Lord and His life-giving Spirit. I know that my Redeemer lives!

A week after the funeral, I had a dream. My Mother appeared to me in the dream in her resurrected body. In her struggle with cancer, her right arm was amputated and she suffered greatly until her death. In the dream, a great light shown before she entered the room, and when I saw her *[I realized that I was in a dream or taken up in the spirit*], her body was completely whole and her youth was restored. I said to her, "Mom, you have your arm!" She replied, "Yeah!" as if to say, "Of Course, I have my arm...in heaven!" Immediately I woke up and I experienced the fullness of a peace that passes all understanding mixed with unspeakable joy. I asked the Lord, what is this...? The answer came in a fullness of knowing as it is written in John 14:1-2:

"Let not your heart be troubled; you believe in God, believe also in Me. In My Father's house are many mansions; if it were not so, I would have told you. I go to prepare a place for you. And if I go and prepare a place for you, I will come again and receive you to Myself; that were I am, there you may be also."

This is a poem I wrote after my Mother's death:

The last day of September
Is the dawning of your first day in this life
As I remember Yesterday
In March was the last day of your life in this world

Seems like an eternity
Seems like I've come through a desert of pain
Looking for one more glimpse of you talking to me
Walking through these rains

Far and away
I hear you letting go of me
Asking for me to do the same
Seek you no more among this temporal plain
For you cannot return to me

One tomorrow I shall see you again
In that place, the Holy One has prepared for us
Till then, both sweet and bittersweet
Memories upon the waves of time
Shall bring to my remembrance
All that I learned at your knee.

I will never forget this visitation. I will always remember the answer to my unspoken prayer. My Mother was absent from me but present with the Lord. There has never been a moment of despair from that day to this. Yet, there is rest available in this life and 1 John 4:17 declares "as He is so are we in this world." Jesus is definitely seated at rest at the Father's right hand, therefore we can be at rest today, now.

When we strive, and press forward in our own efforts and strengths --- God is still and cannot work on our behalf. It is only when we receive and accept that it is not by power or might but by His Spirit that we can rest and place all of our cares at the feet of Jesus where He always heals, comforts, and give us His peace [Zechariah 4:6, Psalm 55:23, 1 Peter 5:7]. We accept that He makes us lie down in green pastures (Psalm 23). That next level comes through the Door of Rest---that is where He leads and restores our souls not to be weary of the battle of the mind. This is especially true after the loss of a loved one...

Do you hear the Voice like the sound of a trumpet blast beckoning you to come through *Heaven's Doorway* to find rest in green pastures?

## MY REFLECTIONS

1. Read Revelation 4. Focus on verse 1.

2. What is God saying to you in this passage? About the *Door of Rest*?
   _____
   _____

3. Why does this Door symbolize a rest we can experience in this world?
   _____
   _____
   _____

4. How does 1 John 4:17 explain the rest that we share with the risen Christ seated at God's right hand?

5. Write the passage in 1 John 4:17 as a declaration and confession?

6. The Door of Rest is a benefit of salvation we can experience today among the living. Explain why?

7. "Come up here, and I will show you things which must take place." What does this mean?

# Reconciliation to God

## Door Keys

### Door Of *Rest*
### *Revelation 4:1 (NKJV)*

"<u>After</u> this I looked, and, <u>Behold</u>, a door was opened
In heaven" and the <u>first</u> voice which <u>I heard</u> was as it were
Of a trumpet speaking with me; saying, '<u>Come up here</u>,
And I will <u>show you things</u> which must take place after this.'"

### *Scriptural Implications:*

1. How long "after"
2. Who opened the "door"?
3. Who was talking?
4. Where is "up here"?

### **Key Words:**
*How do these words frame and focus what God is saying to us through this scripture verse?*

- After
- Behold
- First
- I heard
- Show you things

# Reconciliation Of Others

Our reconciliation of Others to God is Holy Spirit-led, Christ-centered, and God-commanded for our exchange.

# 5

## DOOR OF *WITNESSING*
### Colossians 4:2-3(NKJV)

(Christart, 2015)

*"Continue earnestly in prayer, being vigilant in it with thanksgiving; meanwhile praying also for us, that God would open to us a door for the Word, to speak the mystery of Christ, for which I am also in chains."*

Are you earnest and unwearied and steadfast in your prayer life? Are you being alert and intent in praying and thanksgiving? Are you praying that a "Door of Witnessing" would be open to proclaim the Good News of the Gospel of Jesus Christ? Are you praying that the Great Commission would be realized in these last days?

Paul, the apostle, is the author of Colossians. Paul is a great role model of a life unwearied and steadfast in prayer with thanksgiving. He identifies here in *Colossians 4: 2-3*, the ingredients that should characterize the Christian's responsibility to the great commission to reach the world. We are called to the "ministry of reconciliation" as "ambassadors" for Christ Jesus which means our role aligns with Christ's role. Christ's role was to reconcile and restore all things to Himself, by Him, whether things on earth or things in heaven, having made peace through the blood of His cross (*Colossians 1:20*).

What is the goal? The goal is to pray that God may *open a door to us*, a *"Door of Witnessing"* for the Word to proclaim the mystery concerning Christ, the Messiah. The goal is the "Great Commission" found in Matthew 28:18-20:

*"And Jesus came and spoke to them, saying, "All authority has been given to Me in heaven and on earth. Go, therefore and make disciples of all the nations, baptizing them in the name of the Father and of the Son and of the Holy Spirit, teaching them to observe all things that I have commanded you; and lo, I am with you always, even to the end of the age." Amen.*

The responsibility related to this goal of the "Great Commission" is specific, it is meaningful and measurable to you as the individual Christian (*faith-based believer*), it is achievable, realistic and time-phased (Alan Fine, 2012). What are the consequences if this goal is not reached in the world? It is our common understanding that souls [*people*] will be lost forever and that our Lord desires that none would be lost or perish but that all would come to the saving knowledge of Jesus Christ (*2 Peter 3:9*).

One way that we can join with the Church and the Body of Christ in the earth to ensure that we do our part is to be "unwearied and steadfast in prayer." We can engage in this conversation of intercession wherever we are just as Jesus sits at the right hand of the Almighty God and forever has that same conversation of intercession with Him. Because, as He [Jesus] is, so are we in this world (1 John 4:17). We have access to Almighty God and we sit in Christ at the right hand of the Father God.

We can pray in the spirit [*unknown tongue*], when we do not know how to pray and the Holy Spirit will pray that prayer that avails much by faith through the mysteries of our unknown tongue. The apostle Paul also instructs us in Romans 8:26:

*"Likewise, the Spirit also helps in our weakness. For we do not know what we should pray for as we ought, but the Spirit Himself makes intercession for us with groaning which cannot be uttered."*

I have been praying for the salvation of my husband since 1978, which in 2014 is 36 years. Along the way, in response to my vain repetitions, God has reminded me that He does not save people for my "ease, comfort, and pleasure" but for His glory and the work of His Kingdom. After many years of cries and tears, I recognized by the power of the Holy Spirit to pray for my husband Joe using my prayer language, praying in the Holy Spirit. This way, I never run out of things to bring before the throne of God and my thoughts and emotions are not hijacked from my focus. I know that the Holy Spirit will make my prayers avail much. I pray for my family and each member to experience the fullness of the love of God in the same way. I pray for others and for prayer request that may come in the same way.

> "...that God would open to us a Door for the Word..."

I pray also for laborers – ministers of reconciliation – because the Bible says the harvest is plenty but the laborers are few (Matthew 9:37). This is the cross we must pick-up to follow Christ. Jesus said in John 12:32: "I, if I be lifted up…" Jesus was lifted up on Calvary-

-- therefore we must pray for a Door of Witnessing of the Word to share the gospel of grace and love.

We can believe that the Holy Spirit prays for us and makes our prayers effective when we do not know how to pray effectively (Nelson, 2002). The Spirit-Filled Bible commentary of Romans 8:26 explains, the Holy Spirit's prayer quality control system this way:

*The verse refers to our "groaning" in prayer, then it means that those sighs, groans, loud "cries and tears" (Hebrew 5:7), and other expressions of our hearts and spirits in prayer are taken by the Holy Spirit and made into effectual intercession before the throne of God.*

God speaks through the mouth of man and through the voice of man (Nee, 2014). Jesus was God's Word clothed in human flesh. We are the ministers of God's Word --- Ministers of Reconciliation. God desires to use our mouth and voice to reach others for His kingdom. He could choose anything else in creation but He chose you.

Therefore, let us be so mindful as to continue in prayer and watch also with thanksgiving that God would open wide a Door of Witnessing for the gospel that those in bondage may be free as we are free to come to Christ Jesus through *Heaven's Doorway*!

# MY REFLECTIONS

1. Read Colossians 4. Focus on verse 2-3.

2. What is God saying to you in this passage? About the *Door of Witnessing*?
   _____
   _____

3. Why must witnessing be Holy Spirit-led?
   _____
   _____
   _____

4. Why must witnessing be Christ-centered?
   _____
   _____

5. How is witnessing an exchange for your salvation?
   _____
   _____

6. Why is it necessary to pray that God would open a door for the Word?
   _____
   _____

7. What is your responsibility to God's command to witness?
   _____
   _____
   _____

# Reconciliation to Others

## Door Keys #5

### Door Of *Witnessing*
### *Colossians 4:2-3 (NKJV)*

"<u>Continue earnestly</u> in prayer, <u>being vigilant</u> in it <u>with Thanksgiving</u>; meanwhile praying also for us, <u>that God would Open</u> to us a door for the Word, to speak the <u>mystery Of Christ</u>, for which I am also <u>in chains</u>."

### Scriptural Implications:

1. How should we pray?
2. Is it God's will to open a door for the Word?
3. What is the mystery of Christ? Why is it a mystery?
4. What are the chains? Why is he compelled? Are we compelled as well?

### Key Words:
*How do these words frame and focus what God is saying to us through this scripture verse?*

- Continue earnestly
- Being vigilant
- With thanksgiving
- That God would open
- Mystery of Christ
- In chains

# 6

## Door of *Purpose*
1 Corinthians 16:9 (NKJV)

(Jenson, 2013)

*For a great and effective door has opened to me,
And there are many adversaries.*

Paul, the apostle and the writer of 1 Corinthians, by revelation knew that there was a great and effective door opened to him to preach the gospel of grace in Ephesus. He knew that with that divine call and opportunity there awaited adversaries against his commission. So, Paul announced he would wait. Paul said he would tarry until Pentecost. Paul waited to be endued with power which is a guarantee of effectual service.

By revelation, all who believe in Christ death, burial and resurrection are called to the great commission in Matthew 28. The question is "when" and "how" will the manifestation of power flow. Paul *knew* a "great" a "promising" and "effective" door was wide open to him. Yet, he tarried until Pentecost. He waited on the Lord.

Picture the Indianapolis 500 race, all the powerful cars are lined-up at the starting line, the motors are revving and drivers behind the wheel are anxious to race forward but they wait for the "sound of the gun" to start less they be disqualified by a false start. I believe that our Father God gives us the revelation of the opened door and of the adversaries but we must wait on him to be empowered for the effectual work. Jesus always waited on the Lord and then He opened His mouth and the Holy Spirit filled it (Matthew 5).

Paul's conversation was filled with this sensitivity to the flow of the Holy Spirit throughout the epistles. His language in 1 Corinthian 16 was always one of submission to the flow of the Holy Spirit: *"It may be that I will remain...,"* *"But if it is fitting that I go also...,"* *"if the Lord permits."*

Was Paul fearful of his adversaries and of moving forward and preaching the gospel in Ephesus? No, Paul was not in fear of his adversaries but he knew by revelation, if he was endued with the power of the Holy Spirit, then, no power under heaven could stand against the Gospel of Jesus Christ going forth and many would be saved. Paul would not step out ahead of the leading of the Holy Spirit's power. This is the wisdom of the Door of Purpose. We must be intentional in this call to wait on the Lord. His ways are higher than our ways (Isaiah 55:9).

Paul spoke of his personal plans to go through the wide-open door to preach the gospel he was called to preach to the Gentiles. Yet, he knew as Proverbs 16:9 tells us, "*A man's heart plans his way, but the Lord directs his steps.*" Paul made his plans but he knew that the Lord directed his steps through that door. Proverbs 21:1 also says that our plans are under divine control: "*The king's heart is in the hand of the Lord, like the rivers of water, He turns it wherever He wishes.*" It is God's Holy Spirit who is laying down the pathway for us to follow. According to Romans 8, Paul walked and lived according to the Holy Spirit. Even though, Paul was given the revelation of this wide-open door, he did not rush in haste forward. He waited on the Lord. He knew His God. He only flowed by the Holy Spirit. Paul was purposeful and intentional.

Today, as it was in the day of Paul and the early Church, lives are at stake. Although time is precious to the coming of the Lord, we must be trained to know and understand the leading and timing of the Holy Spirit. Or else, we will do much damage to the souls so desperately in need of salvation.

"A Great and Effective Door..."

I can tell you of my own experience of missing the "when" and the "how" of the leading of the Holy Spirit as I understand it regarding my own husband's salvation and receiving the Holy Spirit with the evidence of speaking in tongues. I was anxious for him to receive all that the Lord had for him as I had received. By revelation, I believed that I knew that a great and effectual door was open unto me to share the Gospel of Grace. My spiritual engine was revving to go! I did not want to leave my husband behind. Yet, my own plans and in my own haste, my steps were not directed of the Lord to force His gift of tongues on my husband. I was not empowered for the work. Only the Lord knows what damage I inflicted on the fledgling soul of my husband, which has diverted his walk until this day. There is therefore no condemnation for God has him in the palm of His hand because the seed has been planted with his acceptance of Jesus Christ as his Lord and Savior. Therefore, I say, "Wait upon the Lord!" (Psalm 27:14) "Wait patiently for Him" (Psalm 37:7). That you might know the purpose of God's will. Jesus waited for God's season and timing. Jesus repeatedly stated to others that His hour had not come. Yet, He knew when His hour had come and demonstrated the greatest witness to the world of how God so loved the world (John 3:16).

The Lord will not tarry to order your steps for it is after all He who has given us this great commission and He is the one whose power opens doors that cannot be shut! (Revelation 3:7-8) Be still and know that I am God (Psalm 46:10), for it is only in stillness will you recognize the still small voice of the Holy Spirit. The Holy Spirit will decide the timing and He will lead you to lead others through *Heaven's Doorway*.

 MY REFLECTIONS

1. Read 1 Corinthians 16. Focus on verse 9.

2. What is God saying to you in this passage? About the *Door of Purpose*?

3. Why is the work of reconciling others to God the Door of Purpose?

4. What are the implications for the Door of Purpose and God's timing for the Ministry of Reconciliation of others?

5. Why is the leading and the power of the Holy Spirit required?

6. What are some consequences of not waiting for the leading of the Holy Spirit?
   _____
   _____

7. How can you practice stillness to hear from God in this and other areas as a Minister of Reconciliation?
   _____
   _____
   _____

# Reconciliation to Others

## Door Keys #6

### Door Of *Purpose*
### *1 Corinthians 16:9 (NKJV)*

For a <u>great and effective</u> <u>door</u> has <u>opened to me</u>,
And there are many <u>adversaries</u>.

### *Scriptural Implications:*

1. Did Paul have some alternative choices?
2. When we understand our purpose and our mission, we can clearly see the opportunities. What was Paul's mission and purpose? What made this a "great and effective door"? What made it a clear opportunity?
3. When we know our purpose, how do we look at oppositions, roadblocks, "Adversaries"?
4. What are the consequences of the going through that "door"?

### **Key Words:**
*How do these words frame and focus what God is saying to us through this scripture verse?*

- Great and effective
- Opened to me
- Adversaries

# 7

## DOOR OF *OPPORTUNITY*
### 2 Corinthians 2: 12-15 (NKJV)

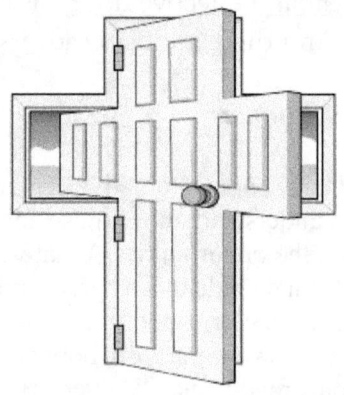

(Christart, 2015)

*Furthermore, when I came to Troas to preach Christ's gospel, and a door was opened to me by the Lord, I had no rest in my spirit, because I did not find Titus my brother; but taking my leave of them, I departed for Macedonia. Now, thanks be to God, who always leads us to triumph in Christ, And through us diffuses the fragrance of His knowledge in every place. For we are to God the fragrance of Christ among those who are being saved And among those who are perishing.*

Paul, an apostle of Jesus Christ by the will of God, is writing this passage as the Lord gave it to me for this devotion. In truth, the passage made no sense to me except that I meditated on the entire chapter in context and studied what Paul said before it and after it. In the passages before 2 Corinthian 2:12-15, Paul is forgiving an offender and in the passage after Paul faces a distraction and anxiety in Troas [*a coastal city of Asia Minor*]. Paul abruptly starts talking about the nature of Christian Ministry and concludes that his experience is just a step in the continuous triumphal procession to the glory of Christ.

*The Roman **triumph** was a victory parade for a conquering army and its leader. Both victors and captives were part of the procession, and both groups could smell the fragrance of burning spices which accompanied the parade. The **aroma**, however, meant something different to each group. Likewise, the fragrance of Christ (the gospel) is to **those who are perishing** an aroma of death leading to death, for it signifies and leads to their ultimate judgment. **Those who are being saved**, find the knowledge of Christ to be an **aroma of life leading to life**, for it signifies life now and leads to life eternal."* (Nelson, 2002)

The eternal destiny of others is a serious matter, as it relates to our charge, to go into the entire world and preach the gospel of Jesus Christ. Paul was distracted at Troas because while he knew the Lord had opened a door for the gospel there…but he left …when he did not find Titus. Titus was a son in the faith to Paul and he was being mentored in the gospel and church leadership. Although, we do not know why Titus was not there when Paul arrived, we know from Paul's letter that he viewed the situation as it related to the commission to preach the gospel of Christ to be a matter of life and death for the eternal destiny of the lost. Yet, rather than to dwell on whether he missed God, Paul used this opportunity and chose to glorify God in Christ Jesus and declared, "Thanks be to God who always leads us in triumph in Christ, and through us diffuses the fragrance of His knowledge in every place."

2 Corinthians 2:11 says, "Lest the devil should take advantage of us, for we are not ignorant of his devices." Paul exercised discernment and emotional intelligence and demonstrated

what our response should be to distractions, test, and things not going as planned. We can continue that victory parade that Jesus began in the pit of hell after His death, burial and resurrection for our salvation taking back the keys to the Kingdom of God. Paul stood and maintained the victory that Christ had already won for us. The devil could have taken advantage of Paul when he arrived in Troas to preach the gospel and did not find Titus because Paul had gone through the open door the Lord provided to him. It could have been a missed opportunity to glorify God in the test of life's disappointments. Titus not showing up was a distraction, a life situation and circumstance. Paul, who sang praises at midnight in the jailhouse, immediately decided it was an opportunity to continue the *victory parade*.

I come from a big family of eight children. Many times, when we have had family gatherings or even when just a few of us had the opportunity to come together, although I recognized the open door, distractions, situations, circumstances at the time kept me from sharing the gospel. Whether that is because I missed it or not, what I learned from this passage, hidden from me in the past -- is in those instances-- if I praise the Lord pass the distractions, *"God always leads us in triumph in Christ, and through us diffuses the fragrance of His knowledge in every place."* I carry the fragrance of the Lord with me where ever I go. The final analysis is

> "For we are to God the Fragrance of Christ..."

we always triumph in Christ and we always have the victory. The fragrance of His knowledge that we carry as living epistles, as the light of the world is in every place that we are in. We do not need to plan to say anything but the Holy Spirit will release and diffuse that aroma, the fragrance of God's love, joy, peace, patience, kindness, goodness, faithfulness, gentleness, and self-control. The beauty of God's loveliness and mercies that are new every morning and that follow us all the days of our lives through Heaven's Doorway are always here and now in its fullness (Lamentations 3:22-23). That door has already been opened to us to share the Gospel of Grace and of God's love today.

Have you been distracted from your Christian purpose to share the gospel of Christ where you are when God clearly has opened a door to you? You are an aroma of life leading to life. As Paul has said, "we are not, as so many, *peddling* the Word of God; but as of *sincerity*, but as from God, we speak in the sight of God in Christ" (2 Corinthians 2:17). There are some who teach the Word of God only as a way of making money or earning a position in the church. I take my charge as a serious responsibility that results in the eternal destiny of others. We have a serious responsibility to share the gospel of Jesus Christ with others and it is a matter of life and death for those who are lost. Stop waiting for a sign! The sign is the cross of Jesus Christ! When the veil was rent in the temple…the door was opened. Use the door of opportunity and go forward knowing you are *more* than a conqueror in Christ Jesus and you are triumphant which means you are dominant in those victories.

The Lord died to open that door of opportunity. So, stay in the state of readiness with your feet shod with the preparation of the gospel. It is a door that no man can shut (Revelations 3:7-8). If an opportunity is thwarted by the devil's devices, strike-up a ***victory parade*** knowing that we always have the victory in Christ Jesus. God's Word is on a mission and it shall never return void but it will succeed its purpose to save as each one enters through *Heaven's Doorway*!

MY REFLECTIONS

1. Read 2 Corinthians 11. Focus on verse 15.

2. What is God saying to you in this passage? About the *Door of Opportunity*?

_____
_____
_____

3. Why did Paul pull back even when the invitation to preach the gospel seem clear?
   _____
   _____

4. What is the lesson in this passage for Ministers of Reconciliation?
   _____
   _____

5. Why should you strike up a triumphant parade in the face of disappointment?
   _____
   _____

6. Think of a time when distractions arose to derail your opportunity to share your testimony. Unpack it using this meditation?
   _____
   _____

7. How is the Door of Opportunity related to reconciliation of others?
   _____
   _____
   _____

# RECONCILIATION TO OTHERS

## DOOR KEYS #7

### *DOOR OF **OPPORTUNITY***
### *2 CORINTHIANS 2: 12-15 (NKJV)*

Furthermore, when I came to Troas to preach Christ's gospel,
And a door was opened to me by the Lord,
I had no rest in my spirit,
because I did not find Titus my brother;
but taking my leave of them, I departed for Macedonia.
Now, thanks be to God,
who always leads us to triumph in Christ,
And through us diffuses the fragrance of His knowledge
in every place. For we are to God
the fragrance of Christ among those who are
being saved and among those who are perishing.

## *Scripture Implications:*

1. Sometimes when we walk in our purpose, we may be in some place for a season. How do we know that a season is changing? What remains unchanged no matter what season you're in?
2. Even though a door was open, Paul departed. What did it mean for Paul to have "no rest in his spirit"?
3. The decision was made based on "no rest" in Paul's spirit? How important is our fellow laborers in Christ?
4. What confidence do we have, when our heart is right with God? Who can lead us to Triumph in spite of ourselves? Why triumph instead of just victory?
5. How important is the knowledge of God? What is the knowledge of God?

6. How should we deal with the fact that our ministry of reconciliation may not always be successful?
7. Who is opening these doors of opportunity?

***Key Words:***
*How do these words frame and focus what God is saying to us through this scripture verse?*

- Always leads us to Triumph
- Fragrance of His knowledge
- Fragrance of Christ.

# 8

# DOOR OF *FAITH*
Acts 14:27 (NKJV)

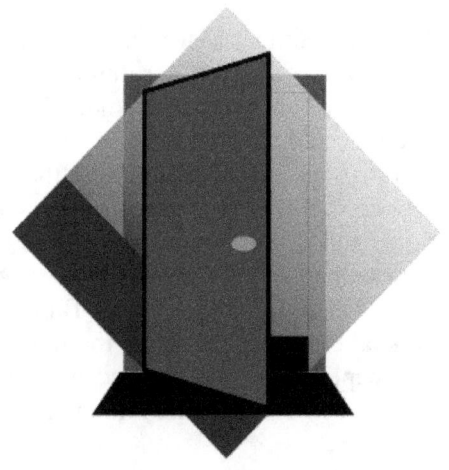

(Doors, 2014)

*And when they were come,*
*and gathered the church together,*
*they reported all that God had done with them,*
*And how He had opened a door of faith unto the Gentiles.*

He opened a door of faith unto the Gentiles. Jesus is the open door of faith that is the light to the Gentiles—we who are not Jews. Paul, the Apostle, in Romans 3:29 says, "Is He the God of the Jews only? Is He not also the God of the Gentiles? Yes, of the Gentiles also." Paul, the Apostle, also writes in Hebrews (v1), "Now faith is the substance of things hoped for, the evidence of things not seen." He further writes (v6) that "without faith it is impossible to please God, for He who comes to God must believe that He is, and that He is a rewarder of those who diligently seek Him." It is important to clarify the terms Gentiles [*a people, nations other than Israel*] and faith [*faith, acceptance, confession of Jesus Christ could save their souls*] (BibleHub, 2014). We must know and understand that a "Door of Faith" was open to the Gentiles because Christ prepared the way for the Gentiles as well as the Jews.

What is the "Door of Faith?" MacLaren's Expository of Acts 4:27 explains, although there are many references in scripture of the "door" metaphor in the New Testament, none is exactly like this. This "door" is connected to the reference in Revelation 3:7-8; the door that is open that no one can shut. Here the door is faith, that is to say faith is conceived of as the means of entrance for the Gentiles into the Kingdom, which, until then, only the Jews had supposed to be entered by hereditary rite [*birth and the rite of circumcision*] (Godvine, 2014). However, Paul and Barnabus on their first missionary tour shattered that notion by the logic of fact of Gentiles being saved and baptized with and filled with the Holy Spirit. By believing in Jesus, Gentiles had come into the Kingdom by the "Door of Faith."

They gathered the church together and they rehearsed all that God had done with them on their mission to the Gentiles. That means they intentionally practiced, went over, ran through, prepared, reviewed, trained, repeated, and studied what God had done for them. (EncartaDictionary, 2009). They reported all God had done. I imagined them telling their stories, giving their testimonies of what God had done with them. They especially told of how God had opened the door of faith to the Gentiles. They realized and were amazed that God was calling the Gentiles in contrast to Israel by grace (Nelson, 2002).

According to the Rainbow Study Bible, the colors of the illustration of the "Door of Faith" at the beginning of this meditation are significant. Purple represents GOD, the Father, the Son, Jesus Christ; the Holy Spirit; the Word of God; Savior; Lord; Messiah; I AM; Lamb of God; King of Kings; and Alpha & Omega. The color green represents LOVE, joy; kindness; mercy; mourning lament; comfort; compassion; peace; sympathy; humility; and charity. This in my opinion translates to John 3:16:

> "For God so loved the world that He gave
> His only begotten Son, that whoever
> believes in Him should not perish
> but have everlasting life."

It is this love, agape, unconditional love, and love by choice and by an act of the will; this is a love unknown to writers outside the New Testament (Nelson, 2002).

As Gentiles, we were part of God's plan for salvation and the "Door of Faith" is opened to us. The question is as Jesus asked the woman at the well, "If you knew the gift of God, and who it is…:"

- Who is standing at the door knocking (Revelation 3:20);
- Who has opened a door in heaven (Revelation 4:1);
- Who has open to you a door of utterance (Rhema) (Colossians 4:2-3);
- Who opened a door to preach Christ's gospel (2 Corinthians 2:11-15);
- Who opened a great and effective door (1 Corinthian 16:9)?
- Who is the door of the sheep where if you enter you shall be saved and shall go in and out, and find pasture (John 10:7-9);
- Who is the Word that will keep a guard before your mouth and keep the door of your lips (Psalm 141:2-4);
- Who is the one we can call on when sin lies at the door and He will provide a way of escape from temptation (James 5:9);
- Who is the one we can call on when the judge stands before the door and we need to forgive and reconcile our brothers and sisters back with God's kind of love (Genesis 4:6-7);
- Who is Who we can call on when we are like a door turning on its hinges not moving ahead or moving too fast (Proverbs 26:14); and
- Who is Who we can call on to put a guard before our mouth and keep the door of our lips speaking out the Word of God as it is

written to keep knowledge on our lips (Psalm 141:2-3, Proverbs 5:2).

The "Door of Faith" is Jesus Christ who gave His life for us and was crucified that "whoever calls on the name of the LORD shall be saved" (Romans 10:13). If you confess with your mouth the Lord Jesus and believe in your heart that God has raised Him from the dead, you will be saved. For with the heart one believes unto righteousness, and with the mouth confession is made unto salvation (Romans 10:8-10).

For this reason, we cannot *"be ashamed of the gospel of Christ, for it is the power of God to salvation for everyone who believes, for the Jew first and also for the Greek" (Gentiles). For in it the righteousness of God is revealed from faith to faith; as it is written, "The just shall live by faith.""* (Romans 1:16). The Door of Faith is wide open and no one can shut it. Therefore, we must be courageous in proclaiming the Gospel of Grace and sharing the love of God abroad. Jesus said, "And I, if I am lifted up from the earth, will draw all peoples to Myself" (John 12:32). This means Jews and Gentiles alike. The battle is not ours and the battle is already won. We must step out in faith and share like the early Christians did in Acts, all that God has done for us.

> "....He had opened a Door of faith unto the Gentiles."

Truth-in-Action in the New Spirit Filled Life Bible (Nelson, 2002) says through John's Gospel we are to let the life of the Holy Spirit bring faith's work alive in us! John's Gospel teaches "godly living is living in, though, and for Jesus. By living godly lives, we learn to see things as God does and adopt His Word as our only standard" (Nelson, 2002). This is the life that is the LIGHT of the world (Matthew 5:14) and when we let that light shine it will draw all men to the Lord Jesus Christ to receive the exceedingly great and precious promises (1 Peter 1:1-4) of God as they enter the Door of Faith. These promises are identified by Charles Stanley of In Touch Ministries (2014) as follows:

1. Our reconciliation to God through the death of Christ (Romans 5:6-10);
2. The daily forgiveness of our sins (1 John 1:9);
3. The Father's continued presence wherever we go (Deuteronomy 31:8);
4. A constant Helper through the indwelling of the Holy Spirit (John 14:16);
5. The Lord's strength in whatever difficulty we face (Isaiah 41:10);
6. God's provision for our daily needs (Matthew 6:25-32);
7. An Answer to our prayers (1 John 5:14-15);
8. The Lord's supply of blessing (Psalm 84:11);
9. The Father's daily help with our burdens (Psalm 68:19);
10. God's comfort in our distress (2 Corinthians 1:3-4);
11. A way of escape when we are tempted (1 Corinthians 10:13);
12. Wisdom for every challenge (James 1:5);
13. Rest for our weary soul (Matthew 11:28-29);
14. Peace regardless of the troubles we face (Philippians 4:6-7);
15. Fruitfulness as we grow older (Psalm 92:12-15);
16. The desires of our hearts (Psalm 37:4);
17. Help in times of trouble (Psalm 46:1-3)
18. Guidance along the pathway of life (Psalm 32:8);
19. Healing for our diseases and wounds (Psalm 103:1-3);
20. The absolute guarantee of God's love (Romans 8:38-39);
21. Eternal security (John 10:27-30);
22. Heaven as our eternal home (John 14:1-3)

The "Door of Faith" is the same as where I began these meditations with Jesus standing at the door knocking. The door of our hearts where Jesus Christ stands knocking swings opens to the inside of our hearts and the Door of Faith swings out and open to the world. We must choose to open the door and accept Jesus as our Lord and Savior and if we do, then the Door of Faith must swing open to the world. We walk by faith not by sight (2 Corinthians 5:7). When we go into our home or when we go into the world (Matthew 5:14, 16), we are the LIGHT of the World and we *must* give that light to the whole house (*in our home*) and we *must* let our light so shine before men (*in the world*), that they may see our good works and glorify our Father in heaven" (Nelson, 2002).

We have the power to influence for good. He who is in you is greater than he who is in the world (1 John4:4). This is the confidence that we must fan the fire of when we witness and share our stories with our family members and with the world. Jesus Christ is the change that they see. Jesus Christ is the love they see. Jesus Christ is the peace that passes all understanding that they see in you in the face of difficult life challenges. Jesus Christ is the understanding that they will see that you can give to someone who can't see the light at the end of the tunnel. Jesus Christ is the hands that you will lay on the sick and they will be healed. Jesus Christ is the joy that you can shed abroad in the hearts of those who can lift up their hands and praise and worship the Lord because you were the epistle that they read and it led them through that open door in heaven that no one can shut.

You are one in a million but still you are one… You cannot do everything but still you can do something. Do not refuse to do the something that you can do (Helen Keller; Edward Everett Hale) to further the gospel and lead the way for someone through the Door of Faith to enter *Heaven's Doorway*!

## MY REFLECTIONS

1. Read Acts 14. Focus on verse 27.

2. What is God saying to you in this passage? About the *Door of Faith*?
   _____
   _____

3. What is the relationship between the Door of Faith and the Door that no one can shut in Revelation 3:7-8?
   _____
   _____

4. Why is gathering together to share what God has done important to your faith?
   _____
   _____

5. Why report, rehearse and practice what God has done?
   _____

6. What does it mean that the Just shall live by faith (Romans 1:16?

7. Why is the Door of Faith important to pleasing God and to receive all the promises of God?

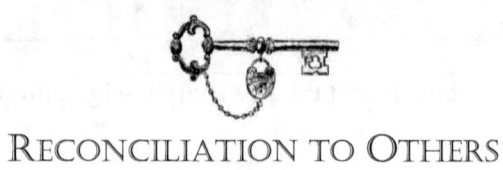

# Reconciliation to Others

## Door Keys #8

### *Door Of Faith*
### *2 Corinthians 2: 12-15 (NKJV)*

<u>And when</u> they were come, and <u>gathered the church</u> Together, they <u>reported</u> all that God had done with them, And how He had opened a door of faith unto the <u>Gentiles</u>.

**Scripture Implications:**

1. Who was Paul accountable to for his work on the mission field? Was this Paul's home church?
2. What was the door of faith? Was there a door of faith open to the Jews?

**Key Words:**
*How do these words frame and focus what God is saying to us through this scripture verse?*

- And when
- Gathered the Church
- Reported all
- Gentiles

# Reconciliation Of Mind

Our reconciliation of Mind is Word-centered for the renewing of our mind, Holy Spirit-driven, for mind/body submission and Fruit-bearing.

# 9

## DOOR OF *INFLUENCE*
### Proverbs 26:14 (NLT)

(Doors, 2014)

*As the door swings on its hinges,
so the lazy person turns over in bed.*

The door swinging on its hinges moves on its hinges but makes no progress beyond its own confined sphere of motion which is about 90 degrees (Godvine, 2014). *In general, we would say that a door "opens" or "closes which would indicate its motion around the hinge* (English & Usage, 2014). Think about it. What is your sphere of motion or influence? Have you confined yourself to your comfort zone which is about 90 degrees? Are you making progress beyond your own confined or self-imposed sphere of motion?

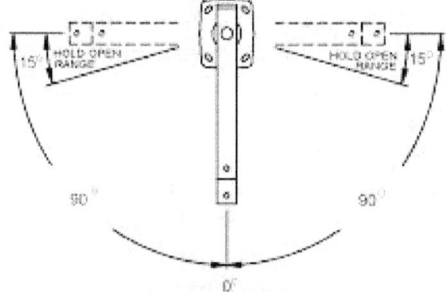

Big doors swing on little hinges. I spent a very long time meditating on this scripture and wondering why the Lord gave me this specific passage for Heaven's Doorway. I read through many commentaries digging to get a revelation of what the Lord was saying to me in this time and season. Meditating I saw "the door swinging on its hinge" compared to the lazy person who turns in his bed is a metaphor or an analogy perhaps for a person remaining in their own comfort zone. Perhaps it is a metaphor for a Christian who is an inactive member of the congregation. Perhaps it is a metaphor of a Christian who never ventures outside of the church walls to share the gospel of grace. Could this be an illustration of a Christian who doesn't understand their role that Christ gave us as Ministers of Reconciliation (2 Corinthians 5:18)? Could this scripture be a metaphor for a Christian who put their light under a basket (Matthew 5:15-16)? Is this scripture a metaphor for a Christian whose salt has lost its flavor? Or could it be a metaphor for a person who doesn't move 180 degrees to repentance? Is it a metaphor for Christians who occupying the pew but never taking any steps to fulfill the call of greatness that Christ died to offer to a dying world? What does it mean to you as a Believer, today?

Well, like all of the scriptures in these writing --- the Lord wanted me to see and share with you that we have to go beyond our own confined sphere of comfort to share the Gospel of Grace. That is why this passage is *the Door of Influence. It could have been the door of Idleness. It could have been the door of diligence. However, my revelation is that it is the Door of Influence for the lazy person who turns over in bed is surely not exercising the gift of influence.*

The *noun influence* is defined as having the capacity to influence the character, development, a behavior of someone or something; the power to cause changes without directly forcing them to happen or the effect itself; the influence of TV violence or social media, music, ideologies, religions, etc. Synonyms are: impact and effect, inspiration, power, authority, determine, guide, control, shape, govern, and decide. (Webster, 2014). The *verb influence* is defined as to have an influence on. An important antonym is "manipulate" or "induce" which is not what we mean here by influence when it is under the power of the Holy Spirit. We are powered by the Holy Spirit like the operating system of a computer coordinating the Fruit of the Spirit. This is the influence which is the consistent sacrifice, focused obedience to the principles of God's Word (Frierson, 2015).

John Maxwell says that Leadership is influence *and that each of us influences at least 10,000 other people during our lifetime? So the question is not whether you will influence someone, but how you will use your influence.* (Maxwell, 2002). The Door of Influence is a powerful anointing in the life of a Believer who accepts the call to greatness.

Jesus said in Matthew 28:18-20, "Go therefore and make disciples of all nations." Jesus also said, it would not be in our own authority but that all authority in heaven and on earth had been given to Him and He would go with us. So, I say to the proverbial lazy person on his bed, what are you waiting for? Are you taking the reasonable steps to satisfy the call of the great commission? "Whoever desires to come after Me, let him deny himself and take up his cross and follow Me" (Mark 8:34).

> Each of us influences 10,000 other people in our lifetime...

What is our sphere of influence or motion (action)? My thoughts are that my sphere of motion is how much I am willing to "act on what I believe?" It is acting on what I believe, by faith. It is how far I am willing to step out on my faith and trust what God has said. Am I willing to share what God has done for me with a love one and point them to the One who saves? Am I willing to trust that Jesus will be with me when I share the love of God with a coworker who is searching for a way forward in the valley of joblessness? Am I willing to let my light so shine before men that they will glorify God? Am I willing to be that light in the darkness of grief for a friend who is wondering where is God in a tragedy? Am I willing to show compassion for a veteran that is struggling to rise from the ashes of war and find a safe haven in a church community? Am I willing to be the salt of the earth in the midst of persecution and rejection by others? Am I willing to listen for the voice of the good Shepherd and to follow Him to find the lost sheep of His pasture? Am I willing to be still and to know it is the Lord standing at the door knocking and take up my cross and follow Him? Who and what are you having an influence or impact?

*Am I willing to bear my soul with you and share a deep disappointment that is humiliating yet in my breaking is a healing balm?* Saleh!

Yes, I am... There are life and times when we are totally oblivious to God's leading to prepare for what is ahead. To be *idle* and unprepared/ under-prepared is to be *lazy*. Influence is taking the reasonable steps of the principles of purpose, prayer, power, and praise, reading and studying the Word of God to keep the oil in our lamps full. Influence is "Whoever desires to come after Me, let him deny himself and take up his cross and follow Me" (Mark 8:34). Matthew 25:1-13 talks about the wise virgins who were prepared and the unwise who were unprepared or *lazy* – *idle* in preparation. I believe that my spirit was asleep at that time and was idle when the pressures of life and circumstances rushed in. Yet, the Lord in His mercy delivered me from my own destruction and all of my troubles (Psalm 103).

Reflecting on *Reconciliation of my Mind* and the *Door of Influence*... In 2011, my husband, Joe, was forced to retire after his job of 24 years was outsourced to Mexico. This began a string of events that marked the tests of life's disappointments, major changes, illness, character and faith. During that year, I began experiencing severe panic attacks driving 50 miles from Saginaw to my job in Flint,

Michigan. In the fall, I had major surgery and struggled to fully recover getting back on the road to work. I lost my focus and concentration to make an impact. Where was my power in the things of God? It takes only a *nanosecond* to follow the fiery dart of a thought and the emotion attached to it into the dark night of the soul.

I was struggling to stay in faith. In January of 2012, although I completed a second master's degree (a *world* success), I made the decision to leave my administrative job and to unconsciously *run away* from my fears or perhaps unknowingly to avoid my call to greatness. Instead I ran to the safety of my family and my home. This safe haven did not last for there is only one safe haven and it is *God's will* as our refuge and fortress. Through a chain of events of unemployment and after spending my retirement to try to keep our home of more than 20 years --- my husband became very ill and was hospitalized with no health insurance

> "As the Door swings back and forth on its hinges..."

--- and we chose to *walked away*, though at the time, we did not understand this disappointment and all the distractions as an opportunity at the *Door of Influence for reconciliation to God and of mind*... During those days my life was as a door swings back and forth on its hinges as I turned over in my bed. W. Clements said, "Big doors swing on little hinges." We have the power to be great influencers in our own lives and in the lives of others…but the little hinges of circumstances derail us sometimes.

As the spiritual one of the family, I did not discern the influence of joblessness and unemployment or the identity crisis caused by my attachment to the world's view of job titles, education titles, neighborhood status that followed. Stripped of all that the world's security offered, it was in this place of brokenness that lead me to retreat at the feet of Jesus to advance to the plans God had for my life (Jeremiah 29:11). Jeremiah goes on in verses 12-13 to say, "Then, you will call upon Me, and you will come and pray to Me and I will hear and heed you. Then you shall seek Me and find Me; when you search for Me with all your heart, I will be found by you, says the Lord..." God had not left me, He had not forsaken me but was there watchfully and affectionately caring for me (1 Peter 5:7).

At the feet of Jesus, I casted all my cares, I brought every thought and every high thing that exalted itself against the knowledge of God, into captivity to the obedience of Christ (2 Corinthians 10:3-6). I learned that I must be diligent to watch and discern the source of every thought --- especially of sudden fear. The perfect love of God **casts out** fear, because fear has torment (1 John 4:18). I had to get up from my bed of idleness and exercise the very power, authority and influence that raised Jesus from the dead.

Through the influence of prayer, praising and worshiping God, sitting under the ministry of the Word at my Church, I was able to stand on my faith. God has provided for my husband and me, a place of refuge with supernatural blessings that could come from no other hand than the hand of God by His mercy and grace. I know who I am and whose I am in Christ because of the influence of the Word of God. I know who my source is as a result. I have plowed through all those distractions. The fear that the devil tried to use as

> "...the Lazy Person turns over in bed."

his device to destroy me and have me curse the Lord failed --- as Job declared, *"Though He sleigh me, yet will I trust Him"* (Job 13:15). I still have a praise inside of me --- therefore a triumphant parade is continual for *nothing can separate me from the love of God which is in Christ Jesus and in all these things we are more than conquerors through Him who loved us* (Romans 8:37-39).

This is the influence that works out our salvation and that is in the trying of our faith --- which is the *Door of Influence* ---to discern the weapons of distractions that form through the trappings of this world and the disappointments it brings. The *cares of the world and the lust of other things* had lulled me into a lazy person turning over in my bed of cares and I was found with my lamp going out of oil when I should have had *oil to spare* by consistently cultivating the Word of Influence that is able to ignite my faith. Psalm 23 talks about our cup running over. With a full lamp and oil to spare, we can lift the banner of our call to greatness and share our story of a triumphant victory parade that is the opportunity standing by for us to act on what we believe and then share our story as God's Ministers of Reconciliation to others. That is the power and influence of my testimony of my recent path to reconcile my mind to God in submission to His will by the leadership of the Holy Spirit for His service and that has led to the completion of these meditations of *Heaven's Doorway*.

My prayer is that if you find yourself turning over on your bed of circumstances (myself included) tossing to and fro --- as a door swings on its "little" hinges --- Remember that Christ dwells in our hearts through faith; "that you, being rooted and grounded in love, may be able to comprehend with all the saints what is the width and length and depth and height --- to know the love of Christ which passes knowledge; that you may be filled with all the fullness of God" (Ephesians 3:17-19). It is the love of Christ which He demonstrated on the cross and that is the gift of God that diligently *compels* us to use the gift of influence with those whose eyes are being blinded to the Gospel of Grace. It is only when this love which passes understanding overflows in our hearts like the oil of a lamp that we are able to give ourselves away in leadership of the Holy Spirit as an influencer. It is love overflowing that brings about our in*fluence to pierce the heart of man not by might not by power but by His Spirit*. Let us use this power of influence to seek and allow the light of the glorious Gospel to shine through us to save the lost because we know first-hand, what God has done for us. Remember, there is a big Door of Influence that no man can shut.

Matthew Henry's Concise Commentary (BibleHub, 2014) of Proverbs 26:14 says, "the slothful man (lazy) hales everything that requires care and labor. But it is foolish to frighten ourselves from real duties by fanciful difficulties." Just know, you are equipped and anointed for this excellent work (2 Timothy 2:21). The harvest is plenty but the laborers are few. Make an impact! Be persistent, focused, purposeful and intentional to accomplish the great commission.

Make an impact in your sphere of influence beyond your comfort zone! What are you waiting for? Get out of your comfort zone bed and go beyond your sphere of motion and seek the lost in your everyday sphere of influence. Share your testimony stories. The time is now! The lost cannot afford to wait another moment to enter *Heaven's Doorway.*

## MY REFLECTIONS

1. Read the Proverbs 26. Focus on verse 14.

2. What is God saying to you in this passage? About the *Door of Influence*? _____
   _____

   How is the *Door of Influence, like a door that swings back and forth on its hinges,* and like the lazy person who turns over in bed related to Reconciliation of our Mind to God?
   _____
   _____

3. What are the steps you need to take to be make an impact?
   _____
   _____

4. What can you SAY or confess that is written from the Word of God to activate your faith?
   _____
   _____
   _____

5. Explain the metaphor of a Christian as the salt of the earth but who has lost their flavor as it pertains to influence?
   _____
   _____
   _____

6. How can the idleness of a comfort zone be laziness and how can this result in being unprepared for life's tests?
   _____
   _____
   _____

# Reconciliation of Mind

## Door Keys #9

### Door Of *Influence*
### *Proverbs 26:14 (NLT)*

As the door <u>swings back and forth</u> on its <u>hinges</u>,
So the <u>lazy person</u> turns over in <u>bed</u>.

### *Scripture Implications:*

1. Is procrastination laziness?
2. What is the standard for "laziness"?
3. Why does Proverbs describe laziness?
4. Is laziness a pattern?
5. What does it mean to swing back and forth on its hinges?

### *Key Words:*
*How do these words frame and focus what God is saying to us through this scripture verse?*

- Swings back and forth
- Hinges
- Lazy person
- In Bed

# 10

## DOOR OF *CHOICE*
### Genesis 4:6-7 (NKJV)

(Doors, 2014)

So the Lord said to Cain,
"Why are you angry?
And why has your continence fallen?
If you do well, will you not be accepted?
And if you do not do well, sin lies at the door.
And its desire is *for you*,
*but* you should *rule over it*."

"Sin lies at the door and its desire is for you, but you should *master* over it." The Spirit-Filled Bible's commentary for this passage says, *sin crouches or hides at the door*. The language virtually personifies sin as a demon crouching like a crazed animal at Cain's doorstep (Nelson, 2002). When the devil attacks, we are like prey to him but the Bible says and we are not ignorant of his devices. What does this mean? How is it that Cain's emotions completely hijacked his rational thoughts and then his actions to murder his own brother?

This appears to be a door of choice and our faith walk is choice-driven. The Lord himself warned Cain and alerted Him to the danger of the arguments and the high thing that *he contemplated* which exalted itself against the knowledge of God [*2 Corinthians 10:4-6*]. That high thing may have been pride because Cain knew the way he should walk in. God coached Cain about the conversation that was brewing in his mind and infecting his heart and showing up in his behavior. In the Scripture, it is evident that Cain was visibly taking steps in the path to anger and his continence had fallen. God reminded him that he knew the right choice that lay before him and he knew how to do the right thing and not to fall into sin. Cain had an opportunity to get it right. Sin desired to rule over him but the right choice would have renewed his mind to master over it.

James 1:9-16 (AMP) spells out for us the process of temptation that leads us into sin, that sin which lies at the door and desires to "rule over" us. Nevertheless, we can choose:

*Blessed is the man who endures temptation; for when he has been approved, he will receive the crown of life which the Lord has promised to those who love Him. Let no one say when he is tempted, "I am tempted by God:" for God cannot be tempted by evil, nor does He Himself tempt anyone. But each one is tempted when he is **drawn away by his own desires and enticed**. Then, **when desire has conceived**, it **gives birth to sin**; and sin, when it is **full grown, brings forth death**. Do not be deceived, my beloved brethren.*

The devil had planted a seed of anger that was based in fear in Cain's mind. When the process of temptation was full grown, the desire of that anger enticed Cain to kill his brother. Temptation is not that sin that lies at the door: we must be alert, recognize we are under attack, nip temptation in the bud, not allow it to be conceived, and give birth to sin.

Life is choice driven. The Bible and the Holy Spirit are always giving us our options and the conditions and the consequences of the choices we have before us. When we are faced with life's temptations and choices be reminded of 1 Corinthians 10:13:

*No temptation has overtaken you except such as is **common to man**; but God is faithful, who **will not allow you** to be tempted beyond what you are able, but will with the temptation will also **make the way of escape**, that you may be **able to bear it**."*

There is an escape doorway built-in to every temptation. However, we may not know that unless we study the Bible and become a student of the Bible while sitting under teaching of a pastor at a local church. Getting saved is not the end of the journey. We must be taught and become equipped with the Word of God. We must know and understand the promises that God has given us in the New Covenant which is our inheritance as Christians. We must not remain ignorant of devil's devices, strategies and plans to lead us into temptation and thereby entice us to sin.

> "If you do well, will you not be accepted?"

We can be sure that sin is crouching at the door desiring to rule over us. However, we can also assume that we are able to master every temptation that is common to man and rule over sin in our lives. It is a choice that we make at the beginning of the test of our faith. The devil begins with a thought and it snowballs to a stronghold. Therefore, we must check our thoughts against the Word of God. This is the way we can rule over sin and master it by recognizing that the weapons of our warfare are not worldly but are mighty in God for pulling down strongholds [structures of thoughts], casting down arguments and every high thing that exalts itself against the knowledge of God, bringing every thought into captivity [detention, custody] to the obedience of Christ (2 Corinthians 10:5) (Nelson, 2002).

In the fall of 1970, I was 18 years old and in my sophomore year at the University of Michigan, Ann Arbor, Michigan. I was attending on a full scholarship. Little did I know that sin was crouching at my door like a crazed animal and its desire was for me. I was tempted and I was enticed and succumbed (chose) to known sin. I had sex outside of marriage and became pregnant. I had an illegal botched-up abortion at the age of 19 in January of 1971. Afterwards, I went about aimlessly for eight years, wounded, rejected, unsaved, in fear of God's wrath for what I had done as a wrong believing Catholic. The self-condemnation that followed nearly stole my life. I didn't know about the saving grace, forgiveness and unconditional love of God.

In 1978, two weeks before my wedding, I accepted Jesus as my Lord and Savior and that began the healing process with right believing. The condemnation did not begin to be released until years later in 2012 when I came to HIS Restoration Ministries a shelter for homeless pregnant women in Saginaw, Michigan.

By faith, I believe that I had a baby girl and it was through the ministry of Ann Fowler that I named her, ReJeanne [*a name I had chosen when I was pregnant with my son, we named Joseph*]. I am at peace and I know that I am forgiven and that I am the righteousness of God through Christ Jesus. My sin is in the sea of forgetfulness and when God looks at me He sees me as the righteousness of Christ Jesus through His precious blood. I know and believe that abortion was nailed at the cross and covered by the redemptive blood of Jesus and that God sees me through the filter of the shed blood of Jesus, my Lord and Savior, my Deliverer, my Healer.

I can speak to women who contemplate abortion because I have experienced the side-effects of years of condemnation and the rejection and abuse of self. I can also speak to the spirit of fear that desires to replay a house of thoughts in our minds. I am a living witness why abortion is not the way. Choose life for yourself and your unborn child and God will make a way out of no way. I fell into sin because I had no Lord and Savior and I was ignorant of the saving grace of God. Don't allow others to influence you in making this decision. I know that we can rule over the sin of abortion because God is a refuge and a fortress and has made a way of escape (1

Corinthians 10:13). I minister to women today who rule over it in spite of being homeless. Sin does not have dominion under grace.

Choice is the product of free will and it is an authority and power that we possess over all of God's creation which is in the likeness and image of God though we are not gods. Let us reflect on the fact that unlike God we are confined in time and place and with it to consequences of our choices. Therefore, our choices must be intentionally considered for their consequences to ourselves, to others, to our families and all who are in our circle of influence as well as in our environment both externally and internally. Choice therefore is not free as our wills are free. Therefore, choose wisely.

James 1:13-16 unpacks and dissects the process of temptation to sin or the choice to sin. God does not want us to be ignorant but God desires to equip each of us with the Word of God. We can rule over sin and Master it but we must be clear that temptation is not sin; the process of sin begins with temptation and the seed of desire but it is our choice alone which leads to and is sin. Be attentive to the voice of God and the voice of your spirit and your thoughts which will warn you about the sin that lies at the door. Chances are…you already know what sin may lie at the door.

Heaven's Doorway offers a way of escape from every temptation that you may be able to bear it and rule over it (I Corinthian 10:13). At the Door of Choice, the executive decision to choose is yours alone. Call upon the name of Jesus, He is *Heaven's Doorway*!

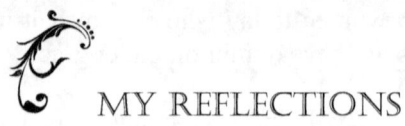
## MY REFLECTIONS

1. Read Genesis 4. Focus on verses 6-7.

2. What is God saying to you in this passage? About the *Door of Choice*? _____
   _____

3. Is there a sin that lies at the door that so easily besets you?
   _____
   _____

4. What scriptural action will you take to rule over it and master it? _____
   _____

5. Read Matthew 4: 1-1-11. What was Jesus' strategy to overcome temptation? _____
   _____

6. Write a scriptural declaration to renew your mind, Begin with, **"It is written.**_____
   _____
   _____

7. Life is response-driven and our responses are choice-driven. How and why is sin choice-driven? Are you choosing death or life today? _____
   _____
   _____
   _____

# RECONCILIATION OF MIND

## DOOR KEYS #10

### *DOOR OF CHOICE*
### *GENESIS 4:6-7 (NKJV)*

*<u>So</u> the Lord <u>said</u> to Cain, "Why are you <u>angry</u>?
And why has your continence fallen?
If you do well, will you not be <u>accepted</u>?
And if you do not do well, sin lies at the door.
And its <u>desire</u> is for you,
But you <u>should</u> rule over it."*

**Scripture Implications:**

1. Why was Cain angry? Who was he angry at? Or what was he angry about?
2. What did Cain have to do "well" to be "accepted"
3. The door is a metaphor for what?
4. What "sin" is desiring to get Cain?
5. What encouraging word did God give Cain?

**Key Words:**
*How do these words frame and focus what God is saying to us through this scripture verse?*

- So
- Said
- Angry
- Accepted
- Desire
- Should

# 11

## Door Of *Utterance*
### Psalm 141: 2-3 (NKJV)

(Kratochvil, 2015)

*Let my prayer be set before You
as incense, and the lifting up of my hands
as the evening sacrifice.
Set a guard, O LORD, over my mouth;
Keep watch over the door of my lips.*

The orders for sentry duty posted at the Queen's London Palace makes it clear that the sentry may not eat, sleep, smoke, stand easy *(at easy)*, sit or lie down during the tour of duty (Wikipedia, 2014). The sentry is not just for show but the guard was trained to do battle. David in Psalm 141:2-3, went to the Lord of Lords, the King of Kings -- God and asked that He would *set a watch before his mouth and keep the door of his lips*. Why would David take such extreme measures and not depend on his own will power? It is Psalm 141, verse 4 that gives us some insight into why David called upon the Lord, *"Incline my heart not to submit or consent to any evil thing, or be occupied in deeds of wickedness with men that work iniquity, and let me not eat of their dainties" (AMP)*. God talking to Moses when he doubted his own ability to speak for the Lord said (Exodus 4:11-12):

> *So the Lord said to him, "Who has made man's mouth?*
> *Or who makes the mute, the deaf, the seeing,*
> *or the blind? Have not I, the Lord? Now therefore,*
> *go and I will be with your mouth*
> *and teach you what you shall say."*

God ordained the power and influence of our tongue so that we can be a witness for Him in the uttermost parts of the earth. Therefore, we dare not use this power and influence for deeds of wickedness.

James, the author of his name sake book of the Bible, who was thought to be the Lord Jesus' brother, talks about the untamable tongue. James 3:1-12, reports (v.5) that the tongue is a little member but its power and influence for good or bad are out of proportion to its size (Nelson, 2002). James says (v.6), the tongue is a fire, a world of iniquity and it is set on fire by hell, (v.8) no man can tame the tongue; it is an unruly evil, full of deadly poison. With it we bless our God and Father, and with it we curse men, who have been made in the similitude of God (v.9). Out of the same mouth proceed blessings and cursing (v.10). My brethren, these things ought not to be so (v.10). As a result, David sought the Lord to stand a guard before his mouth and to keep the door of his lips. David did not dare say anything that the Lord had not put in his mouth to speak.

We open our lips to open our mouths, thus our lips are the door and it is our tongue that allows us to speak. The National Center for Biotechnology Information at the U.S. Library of Medicine (2013) indicates that humans use the tongue's movability for speaking. Only when tongue, lips and teeth work together do sounds from the throat turn into understandable letters and words. The tongue is extremely agile and quick: It can produce more than 90 words per minute, using more than 20 different movements. The tongue is essential for speaking and to produce understandable sounds and words in any language.

The Bible recognizes the power and the influence of the tongue in James 3:6 and states it is *"able to defile the whole body."* Proverbs 21:23 declares *"whoever guards his mouth and tongue keeps his soul from trouble."* 1 Peter 3:10, says, *"He who would love life and see good days, let him refrain his tongue from evil, and his lips from speaking deceit."* James 1:26 declares, *"if anyone among you thinks he is religious, and does not bridle his tongue but deceives his own heart, this one's religion is useless."* Psalm 34:13 says, *"Keep your tongue from evil, and your lips from speaking deceit."* Proverbs 18:21 declares, *"Death and life are in the power of the tongue, and those who love it will eat its fruit."*

The New Spirit-Filled Life Bible commentary (Nelson, 2002) for Proverbs 18:21 tell us, a person's life largely reflects the fruit of his tongue. To speak life is to *speak God's perspective* on any issue of life, to speak death is to declare life's negatives, to declare defeat, or complain constantly. We speak death to the life around us when we slander; Psalm 50:20 says, "you sit and speak against your brother; you slander your own mother's son." We make false accusations when *the devil* uses the tongue in our mouths to lie against one another and bear false witness; Amos 7:10 says, "Amos has conspired against you in the house of Israel. *The land is not able to bear all his words."* We gossip and are talebearers, backbiting against our neighbors; Proverbs 11:13 says, *"A talebearer reveals secrets, but he who is of a faithful spirit conceals a matter."* Psalm 15:1-3 declares the character of those who dwell with the Lord in His tabernacle (*in His presence*) is he who does not backbite with his tongue. In Matthew 12:31, Jesus speaks about the "unpardonable sin" and it is speaking against the Holy Spirit, and that sin will not be forgiven in this age or the age to come. The commentary explains that the Pharisees' slander of the Holy Spirit was not merely an

utterance of the lips but an expression of character. It is written in Isaiah 6:5:
> "Woe is me, for I am undone! Because I am a man
> of unclean lips. And I dwell in the midst of a people
> Of unclean lips..."

Then, a seraphim, touched his mouth and said,
> "Behold, this has touched your lips; your iniquity
> Is taken away, and your sin purged."

We need to recognize the status of our mouth and lips because in the presence of God we also will be undone as Isaiah was but the Lord provided atonement and cleansing because Isaiah had a contrite heart.

The Bible mentions the "mouth" 423 times in the King James Version (KJV, 2014). There is a flattering mouth (Proverbs 26:28); an immoral mouth (Proverbs 22:14), a pompous mouth (Daniel 7:8), a judging mouth (Luke 19:22), a mouth and wisdom that all your adversaries will not be able to contradict or resist (Luke 21:15), and there are grumblers, complainers who mouth great swelling words to gain advantage (Jude 16). Finally, there is the mouth of God. Lips are also mentioned in the Bible 85 times. There are lying lips (Psalm 120:2) bridled lips (2 Kings 19:28), lips testifying against you (Job 15:6, lips to do evil (Leviticus 5:4), perverse lips (Proverbs 4:24), and lips that speak guile (1 Peter 3:10).

> "Keep watch over the Door of my lips."

If we do not seek to restrain our tongue and to pray that the Lord would set a guard before our mouths and keep watch over the door of our lips, how shall we dwell in the secret place of the Most High God? How can we be living Epistles? How can we be the Lord's Ambassadors and the Lord's Ministers of Reconciliation? How can we be witnesses who carry and bring the Gospel of Grace, Peace and Love to our families, friends, community, the circle of our influence and the world?

How shall we restrain our tongue, set a guard before our mouth, and keep the door of our lips? Matthew 12:33 declares that a tree is known by its fruit or a man is known by his word; (v.34) "How can you, being evil, speak of good things? For *out of the abundance of the heart the mouth speaks.*" The Pharisees in Matthew 12 rejected the truth concerning Jesus, rejected the truth from the words and deeds of Jesus and deliberately chose to insult the Holy Spirit (Nelson, 2002). This points to our need according to Romans 12: 1-3 to become living sacrifices. Paul declares, in light of the great plan of salvation and particularly all the mercies and benefits it brings to us as Believers, let us respond by renewing our minds and committing ourselves to the ideals of the Kingdom of God (Nelson, 2002). In 1 Corinthians 9:23, 27, Paul says, "Now this I do for the gospel's sake, that I may be partaker of it with you (v.23)." And he goes on to say (v.27), "I discipline my body and bring it into subjection, lest, when I have preached to others, I myself should become disqualified."

What are those ideals? When our minds are renewed by listening to the Man of God preach and teach the Word of God, by reading and studying the Bible, by listening to Bible-driven teachings on CD's and reading Bible-driven books, and/or listening to the Bible on tapes/CD's / or MP3 players etc.; our mind *synchronize with* our spirits and in agreement the *"sprit/mind/body"* out of the abundance of the well-spring of our heart (*spirit*), we will only speak God's perspective. *This brings into harmony our tripartite being in a harmonic symphony of faith that can move mountains and release miracles.* When we think and meditate on whatever things are true, whatever things are noble, whatever things are just, whatever things are pure, whatever things are lovely, whatever things are of good report, if there is any virtue and if there anything praiseworthy – we are to meditate on these things (Philippians 4:8). The fruit of our character then becomes what Galatians 5:22-23 describes as the Fruit of the Spirit, which are; love, joy, peace (*concerns our attitude towards God),* patience, kindness, goodness (*deals with social relationships*), faithfulness, gentleness self-control (*guides our Christian's conduct*) (Nelson, 2002).

Whatever situation or issue David was facing when he wrote Psalm 141 he knew he needed supernatural control over the power of the tongue. David knew that it was not by power and not by might but it was by the Spirit (Zechariah 4:6) that he would be able to bridle his tongue, and therefore, he sought the Lord. In Zechariah 4:6, God informs the rebuilder of the temple that the task would not be accomplished through the force of an army or through muscular power or physical stamina of workmen; rather it would be accomplished by the empowering of the Spirit of God (Nelson, 2002). In the same way, since we are the temple of the Holy Spirit, as we renew our minds with the Word of God, we are in a sense rebuilding our temple not by our own will power but by the empowering of the Holy Spirit. When we pray in the Spirit in our unknown tongue, we are rebuilding our temple and strengthening its walls. The Holy Spirit is the guard that is set before our mouth and who keeps the door of our lips through the fruit of the Spirit that guides our Christian Conduct to be faithful with our words, gentle in the attitude and spirit of our words, and self-controlled in the choice of our words.

As I was growing up, I apparently always said what I was thinking. It was not always appropriate or tactful. Sometimes, I can hear my Dad's voice in my head saying, "Girl, you cannot always say what you are thinking!" As a young adult in my twenties, I use to be sarcastic. Sarcasm is defined as a cutting often ironic remark intended to wound, or a form of wit that is marked by the use of sarcastic language and is intended to make its victim the butt of contempt or ridicule (Dictionary, 2009). As I grew older, I accepted the Lord and ended the sarcasm and became more direct in the way I communicated. However, at work I was told that I was intimidating and that I needed to soften my remarks and smile. I also realized that some of my remarks were judgmental. I was always feeling like "Me and my BIG mouth" or "Misunderstood." This has had the effect of silencing my voice because the desire of my heart is to communicate in ways people can accept and understand. When I was teaching the new members class on faith at my home church, I was accused of saying something that may have confused a new member –but I was never told what specifically I said. God puts a high accountability on those who teach the Word and I did not want to present a stumbling block to others with my words. While I believe I was misunderstood and misrepresented, these days I practice placing a guard before my mouth to keep the door of my lips.

I really didn't realize the casualties of my tongue when there was no guard. When I became a Christian, I became more and more sensitive to the effects of my words on others and the Lord coached me in gentleness and self-control. I learned that God's emotional intelligence is the nine Fruit of the Spirit and when I focused on these virtues I became more self-aware. I was able to self-regulate my reactions in the face of triggering events and not just say the first thing that comes into my mind. I can display a character of self-control. I became more socially aware and I was able to manage relationships over time. Most importantly, I have learned the need to bridle my tongue as a Minister of Reconciliation. I have learned to withhold judgment because all of our sins were judged on the body of Jesus at the Cross. God alone is our judge.

> "Set a guard, O Lord, over my mouth."

When I replaced the idle chatter that was coming out of my mouth and defiling my lips with the spoken Word of God and the Rhema and Logos Word my life changed forever. I learned as Jesus said when He was tempted, "It is written, "Man shall not live by bread alone, but by every Word that proceeds from the mouth of God.'" (Nelson, 2002) In this way, we can avoid being snared by the words of our mouths and being taken by the words of our mouths (Proverbs 6:2). Instead, by speaking the Word of God (*Rhema*) we "may preserve discretion, and your lips may keep knowledge" (Proverbs 5:2). If our lips keep knowledge because we are speaking aloud the Word of God, what is written, then as Jesus declared in Luke 21:15, "…for I will give you a mouth and wisdom which all your adversaries will not be able to contradict or resist" for a testimony.

Jesus always demonstrated the Fruit of the Spirit, self-control. The virtue of Self-Control is having a *great force within but under control*, the ability to live with restraints (Strand, 2009). The power of life and death are in the tongue but we must keep this great force under control and under restraints. David in Psalm 141 was not born again or saved. David lived under the Law (*10 Commandments*) and he had to seek that support from God in his time of trouble. If we are saved and Spirit-filled, we have the same power of the Holy Spirit that raised Jesus from the dead, living inside of us. We are "fully loaded" and equipped by the Holy Spirit to activate that guard over the door of our lips.

The Holy Spirit will always be that guard before our mouths and will keep the door of our lips. We can also pray in our spiritual language (in tongues) to mobilize our virtue of self-control when we are under attack. We have the power of authority given to us by God to bridle our tongue and bring that member of our body under the control of the Spirit (*as we are led by the Holy Spirit*) by maintaining a renewed mind and uttering the Word. Then, we can open our mouth, like Jesus did while He was on earth and God will fill it and give us the Logos which will lead people to enter *Heaven's Doorway*.

 MY REFLECTIONS

1. Read Psalm 141. Focus on verses 2-3.

2. What is God saying to you in this passage? About the *Door of Utterance*?

3. Do you need to ask the Lord to set a guard you're your mouth and keep watch over the door of your lips? (Self-Assessment)

4. In your daily roles (spouse, parent, child, believer, etc.) what power and influence does your tongue communicate?

5. How would the nature of your communications change if I reminded you that God is always watching?

6. What impact will what you say today have tomorrow, in 30 days, in six months from now, a year from now, or for a lifetime in the lives you influence?
   _____
   _____

7. What does it mean to speak God's perspective?
   _____
   _____

# Reconciliation of Mind

## Door Keys #11

### Door Of *Utterance*
### *Psalm 141:2-3 (NKJV)*

Let <u>my prayer</u> be set before You as incense,
And the lifting up of <u>my hands</u> as the
evening sacrifice. Set <u>a guard</u>,
O LORD, over my mouth;
<u>Keep watch</u> over the door of my lips.

### *Scripture Implications:*

1. Worship sets the atmosphere for what?
2. What does incense signify in worship? What was the evening sacrifice?
3. Why a "guard"? Why a watch?
4. What is the importance of our "mouth"? Our "lips"

### *Key Words:*
*How do these words frame and focus what God is saying to us through this scripture verse?*

- My prayer
- My hands
- A guard
- Keep watch

# 12

# Door of *Judgment*
James 5:8-9 (NKJV)

(Doors, 2014)

*You also be patient. Establish your hearts,
for the coming of the Lord is at hand.
Do not grumble against one another,
Brethren, lest you be condemned.
Behold, the Judge is standing at the door!*

James is calling on Christians to be *patient* with one another. Specifically, "do not grumble against one another." Actually, James begins the Book with a call to patience (*James 1:2-4*):

> *My brethren, count it all joy when you fall into various trials, knowing that the testing of your faith produces patience. But let patience have its perfect work, that you may be perfect and complete, lacking nothing.*

Patience is a fruit of the Holy Spirit (*Galatians 5:22-23*) that is demonstrated when the life of a believer is fully controlled by the Holy Spirit. Of the nine Fruit of the Spirit, patience is one of the second triad: [love, joy, peace| ***patience, kindness, goodness|*** faithfulness, gentleness, self-control], which deals with social relationships (Nelson, 2002). Patience is that character that only the Holy Spirit can produce in a Christian and it is not produced from our own efforts. Patience is a process and James clarifies that it is the "testing of your faith" that produces patience. That testing of our faith that produces patience comes through interactions with one another or through social relationships.

In this passage, the context is that the coming of the Lord is at hand and the judge is standing at the door. Why then must we be patient with one another and specifically, that we should not "grumble against one another." Let's unpack this charge. The definition of the Fruit of the Spirit, "patience" or "longsuffering" is forbearance, long-enduring, fortitude, being able to handle one's anger slowly. The implication is that patience requires character and a type of virtue that is exercised over time and that it may require some discomfort and even pain. *I suggest that "patience" requires a spirit of unity and that is the wisdom of the fruit of patience mixed with the love of God.*

> Therefore, if there is any consolation in Christ if any comfort of love, if any fellowship of the Spirit, if any affection and mercy, fulfill my joy by being like-minded, having the same love, being of one accord, of one mind. Let nothing be done through selfish ambition or conceit, but in lowliness of mind let each esteem others better than himself. Let each of you

look out not only for his own interests, but also for the interests of others.

The character of patience which is unity involves being aware of our own selves as well as being aware of the feelings and emotions of others and determining how we will respond. The Bible in *James 5:8-9* urges us as Christians made in the image and likeness of God to be mindful and intentional about handling our anger slowly with one another. A more instructive passage on the Biblical perspective of patience with one another and its demonstrated capacity for virtue [*love*] and character within the community of faith is *1 Corinthians 13:4-8*:

> *"Love is patient [suffers long] and is kind; love does not envy; love does not parade itself, is not puffed up; does not behave rudely, does not seek its own, is not provoked, thinks no evil; does not rejoice in iniquity, but rejoices in the truth; bears all things, believes all things, hopes all things, endures all things. Love never fails."*

We find that our faith must work through love (*Galatians 5:6*) to allow the Holy Spirit to produce patience in our lives and the glory of this supernatural manifestation of the fruit of the Holy Spirit is that there is no condemnation or bondage attached when we are able to walk in the Spirit of unity. Our faith must be mixed [*Hebrews 4:2*] with the Word of God, our faith can work through love [God is love] and thereby the mystery of the supernatural overflow of patience is the unity we seek that leads to peace.

What does it mean, "The Judge that stands at the door?" The passage begins with the context to be patient and to not grumble against one another, lest you be condemned. *Patience* is a quality of love and we know that God is love and exercises *longsuffering* towards each of us daily and desires to reconcile us to himself in the unity of the Spirit. *Patience* is slow to anger. In fact, it is of the Lord's mercies that we are not consumed because His mercies fail not, they are renewed every morning [*Lamentations 3:22-23*]. That is an indication of how much [*the quantity of*] patience is needed for just one of us. Patience requires "agape" love as a fruit of the Spirit…it requires that we exercise unconditional love. Many times, it is our emotions that hijack our soul [*mind, will, emotions, intellect, imagination*] and circumvent the love and patience we have inside in the abundance of our hearts to give to ourselves and others for reconciliation.

My personality (ego) has a tendency to be judgmental and critical. I am always analyzing situations, circumstances and people in an attempt to understand myself and others. However, when I do that thinking out loud without patience, kindness, goodness, and gentleness (*God's emotional intelligence*), it is sometimes perceived by others as having a judgmental tone. I am aware of this because while I do not see myself as others see me, I have those who are honest with me and tell me that it sounds like I am judging or being judgmental. One of the reasons that I am working on it is that my judgment of others only results in condemnation of myself. Somehow, those judgments manifest in my own life like a boomerang and are turned inward and begin a cycle of condemnation when I find myself repeatedly punishing myself for the same thing I judged in others.

> "Behold, the Judge is standing at the Door!"

For a season, a wedge emerged between my oldest sister, Nadia and I, who had always been my best friends. My Mother always had a buddy system with the eight of us children and paired a younger child with an older sibling. I was paired with my oldest sister, Nadia. When I was growing up, she was that buddy, we slept in the same bed, she dressed me, she made sure I had my bath, and she mentored me as a big sister. When we were grown, it came a time after my Mother died that I questioned the decisions that she made as the Administrator of my Mother's estate and I became judgmental and critical of her along with my other siblings. As a perfectionist, I had expectations for her to be perfect and I judged her. The experience strained our relationship for years until I recognized that I was judging and sought inner healing. She was getting a double barrel because of her own judging ego and in strife, the devil had taken me captive [*hijacked my emotions*] at will and I became the vehicle of the accuser. My desire was to save the relationship in love and that is the *quality of Unity* which grows out of patience.

The judge stands at the door; therefore, we need **not** take on his role or be a messenger of the enemies' lies. The devil is the condemning judge at the door. The devil attacks us by speaking to us directly and by using other people's mouths to judge, humiliate, and shame us (Prince, 2003). The devil attacks us by impersonating our own voice to feed us lies about God and our identity in Christ. God is a God of love and seeks always to save the relationship and therefore we should recognize the deceiver and respond in agape love. *The wisdom of patience is Unity and it is this patience that opens the door of Unity at Heaven's Doorway.*

We lose patience with one another whenever we judge. In the end, there is only one pronounced judge and that judge is Jesus Christ. God has declared that He is the righteous judge and He alone will judge the living and the dead at His appearing and His kingdom (2 Timothy 4:1, 8). Therefore, by faith we must offer supernatural agape love, patience and understanding to one another recognizing that we each will be judged in time and we therefore need not take on that role with one another in this world and life on earth. By withholding judgment, we give way for unconditional love [*agape*] to flow to others and nurture miraculous relationships. Other people in our relationships do not have to live up to our expectations. God alone has set a standard that we all must meet and that is to, "Love one another as I have loved you" (John 13:34). We must not compare ourselves for the Bible says, "But they, measuring themselves by themselves, and comparing themselves among themselves, are not wise" (2 Corinthians 10:12).

> "Do not grumble against one another..."

We must start with self-awareness and self-assessment. Many times, that inner judge that voices judgments in our minds is either our own ego [**E**dging **O**ut **G**od] or the external judge is the devil's voice, which is the accuser of the brethren (Revelation 12:10).

That tormenting judge is not our God nor is it Jesus Christ because God is a merciful Judge and Jesus is a righteous Judge. In Isaiah 54:17b, God declares: "This is the heritage of the servants of the Lord, and their righteousness is from Me." God judged and punished all of our sins past, present and future on Jesus Christ on the Cross and now sees us through His righteousness!

According to 1 John 4:17, **"Love has been perfected among us in this: that we may have boldness in the Day of Judgment; because as He is, so are we in this world."** Judgment has unforgiveness at its roots. Matthew 18:22 shows us a deeper meaning of the quality of patience and why it satisfies unity:

> Then Peter came to Him and said, "Lord, how often shall my brother sin against me, and I forgive him? Up to seven times?" Jesus said to him, "I do not say to you, up to seven times, but up to seventy times seven."

Have you forgiven your sister or brother 490 times? Well, that is the nature of the kingdom of God. That is the character of patience and which is the wisdom of unity. Let us take every thought and project and make it obedient to Christ (2 Corinthians 10:5) "Therefore, let us not judge one another anymore, but rather resolve this, not to put a stumbling block or a cause to fall in our brother's [or sister's] way" (Romans 14:13) but let us point them to *Heaven's Doorway* withholding judgment. *Selah!*

*Proverbs 3:3-4:*
> Let mercy and kindness [*shutting out of hatred and selfishness*] and truth [*shutting out all deliberate hypocrisy and falsehood*] forsake you;
> bind them about your neck, write them
> on the tablet of your heart.
> So shall you find favor, good understanding,
> and high esteem in the sight
> [or judgment] of God and man.

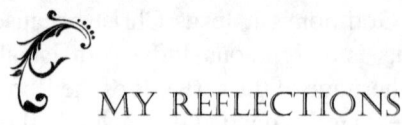

## MY REFLECTIONS

1. Read James 5. Focus on verses 8-9.

2. What is God saying to you in this passage? About the *Door of Judgment*?
   _____
   _____

3. When you hear the word "Judgment" what are the words, pictures, and feelings that bubble up?
   _____
   _____

4. What does it mean in this passage to *ESTABLISH* your heart?
   _____
   _____

5. Who is the Judge standing at the door?
   _____
   _____

6. Why is the coming of the Lord important to whether you grumble against others or not?
   _____
   _____

7. The Judge at the door is God watching you. What kind of Judge is God? Do we condemn ourselves or does God judge us?
   _____
   _____
   _____

# Reconciliation of Mind
## Door Keys #12

### Door Of *Judgment*
### *James 5:8-9 (NKJV)*

You also be <u>patient</u>. <u>Establish</u> your hearts,
For the <u>coming of the Lord</u> is at hand.
Do not <u>grumble</u> against one another,
Brethren, lest you be <u>condemned</u>.
<u>Behold</u>, the <u>Judge</u> is standing at the door!

## *Scripture Implications:*

1. How do you establish your "hearts"?
2. The Lord is going to come! How should we act with this knowledge?
3. Why does "grumbling" lead to condemnation?
4. How should we act knowing who's looking over our shoulder?

## *Key Words:*
*How do these words frame and focus what God is saying to us through this scripture verse?*

- Patient
- Establish
- Grumble
- Condemn
- Behold
- The Judge

# PRAYER OF SALVATION

*Romans 10:9*

*If you confess with your mouth the Lord Jesus
And believe in your heart that God has raised
Him from the dead, you will be saved.*

Lord Jesus, I invite You into my life.

I believe You died for me and that Your blood pays

for my sins and provides me with the gift of eternal life, unmerited

favor and grace.

By faith I receive these gifts, and I acknowledge You

as my Lord and Savior. Amen.

# Afterword

Beloved, it is this trying of my faith that has led to the completion of this book of meditations and the sanctification of the *Gift that is in me*. My goal is to be a door that points to Jesus, Heaven's Doorway.

I pray that you have enjoyed *Heaven's Doorway: Meditations for Ministers of Reconciliation* will continue to enjoy and go back to these meditation as the Lord leads you in the seasons of your life. I encourage to share your testimony with those you meet and even to venture out of your comfort zone to share the Gospel of Grace. By doing this you will bear much fruit of the Spirit.

I want to encourage you to pass this book of Meditations on to others and to continue to grow in the Lord. Ministers of Reconciliation have told me that they have referred back to the mediations as a devotional throughout the year. Use each of the 12 meditations as a monthly reading reflecting on the selected meditation all month long. Share these meditations with evangelism teams before praying to prepare the ground and to reinforce the great commission. Use these meditations as an evangelistic tool and give it as a gift that will keep on giving. It is a God Idea! May the grace of the Lord Jesus Christ, and the love of God, and the communion of the Holy Spirit be with you all, Amen.

I am interested in how Heaven's Doorway impacted your life and the lives of others. Contact me and share your story, it may end up in my next book:

Rose M. Beane, Ph.D.
BLD & Associates, LLC
Wisdom of Excellence

bldassociatesllc@gmail.com

## MEET THE AUTHOR

Rose Margaret Lataillade-Beane, Ph.D was born in Port-au-Prince, Haiti, and was raised in Detroit, along with four brothers and three sisters. In 1957, the Lataillade family became naturalized American citizens. She sits under the teaching ministry of Drs. Ron and Georgette Frierson at New Covenant Christian Center of Saginaw, Michigan.

Dr. Beane is married to Joe Beane, Jr., her husband of 36 years. She has one adult son, Joseph Lee Beane, who is married to Cayla Canelas where they all live in Denver, Colorado.

*1 Timothy 4:14 and 15* keynote the Lord's messages for her life. "Do not neglect the gift this is in you ..." This collection of 12-Meditations for Ministers of Reconciliation by private publication is her third book. Her mission is to equip people according to *Proverbs 20:5 (AMP)*:

> "Counsel in the heart of man is like water in a deep well,
> But a man of understanding will draw it out."

Dr. Beane has a Bachelor of Science from Wayne State University, a Master's in Education from Saginaw Valley State University, a Master's in Psychology with a specialization in Executive Coaching from the University of Rockies, and a Doctorate in Adult Learning from Michigan State University.

Beane is a member of Delta Sigma Theta Sorority. She has Elijah House Prayer Ministry Certification. She volunteers as Assistant Director of HIS Restoration Ministries Maternity Home for homeless pregnant women. Dr. Beane is on staff in higher education.

# SOURCES

# REFERENCES

Alan Fine. (2012). *InsideOut Coaching.* InsideOut Development, LLC.

BibleHub. (2014, August 12). *Bible Hub.* Retrieved from Bible Hub: Acts 14:27: http://biblehub.com/commentaries/acts/14-27.htm

Bradberry, T., & Greaves, J. (2009). *Emotional Intelligence 2.0.* San Diego: TalentSmart.

Christart. (2015, April 7). *Christart.com.* Retrieved from www.christart.com

ClipartOf. (2015, March 25). *www.ClipartOf.com.* Retrieved from ClipArtOf: http://www.clipartof.com//84926

ClipArtOf. (2015, 30 2015). *www.ClipArtof.com.* Retrieved from http://ClipartOf.com/69881

Dictionary, T. F. (2009). *Sarcasm.* Retrieved from The Free Dictionary by Farlex: http://www.thefreedictionary.com/sarcasm

Doors, G. (2014, July 23). *Images of Open Doors, Google.* Retrieved from Images of Open Doors: https://www.google.com/search?q=open+doors

EncartaDictionary. (2009). *Encarta Dictionary: English (US).* Microsoft.

English & Usage. (2014, November 17). *English & Usage.* Retrieved from English & Usage Stack Exchange: http://english.stackexchange.com/questions/92449/what-does-a-door-do-on-its-hinge

Frierson, R. (2015, March 3). Heaven's Doorway. (R. Beane, Interviewer)

Godvine. (2014, August 12). *Godvine.* Retrieved from Godvine: http://www.godvine.com/bible/acts/14-27

Goleman, D. (2006). *Working with Emotional Intelligence.* New York, NY: A Bantam Book.

Images of Revelation. (2014, July 23). *Images of Revelation.* Retrieved from http://www.imagesofrevelation.com/revelations/images/jesus_at_door.jpg

Jenson, J. (2013, June 27). *Somusing*. Retrieved from http://erin.zayda.net/2013/06/church-of-st-giles-burnby.html

KJV, K. J. (2014, August 16). *Online King James Version, Official Site*. Retrieved from http://www.kingjamesbibleonline.org/

Kratochvil, P. (2015, March 24). *Public Domain Picture*. Retrieved from Buckingham Palace Guard: http://www.publicdomainpictures.net/view-image.php?image=7785&picture=buckingham-palace-guard

Maxwell, J. (2002). *Leadership 101: What ever leader needs to know*. Nashville, TN: Thomas Neslon Publishers.

NCBI. (2013, January 1). *How does the tongue work?* Retrieved from National Center for Biotechnology, U S National Library of Medicine: http://www.ncbi.nlm.nih.gov/pubmedhealth/PMH0033703/

Nee, W. (1965). *The Release of the Spirit*. Indianapolis, Indiana: Sure Foundation.

Nee, W. (2014). *Spiritual Discernment*. New York: Christian Fellowship Publishers, Inc.

Nelson, T. (2002). *New Spirit-Filled Life Bible*. Nashville, TN: Thomas Nelson Publishers.

New Tribes Mission. (2015, March 29). *New Tribes Mission*. Retrieved from New Tribes Mission Photos: http://usa.ntm.org/mission-videos-and-mission-photos

Oxford, D. (2014, December 1). *Oxford Dictionary*. Retrieved from Oxford Dictionary: http://www.oxforddictionaries.com/definition/american_english/due-diligence

Prince, J. (2003). Wining the Battle against fear, guilt & addiction: Spiritual warfare myths and truths #2 - smite your ites'. Singapore.

Stanley, C. (2014, August 16). *In Touch Ministries*. Retrieved from In Touch Ministries: http://www.intouch.org/you/article-archive/content/topic/god_s_precious_promises_article#.U-_tlPldXw8

Strand, R. (2009). *Nine Fruit of the Spirit:A Bible Study on Developing Christian Character:Love, Joy, Peace, Patience, Kindness, Goodness, Faithfulness, Gentleness, Self-Control*. Green Forest, AR: New Leaf Press.

The Foundation Lockman. (1987). *The Amplified Bible.* Grand Rapids, Michigan: Zondervan.

Warren, R. (2004). *What on Earth Am I Here for? From The Purpose Driven Life.* Grand Rapids, MI: Zondervan.

Webster, M. (2014, December 1). *Merriam Webster.* Retrieved from Merriam Webster Dictionary: http://www.merriam-webster.com/dictionary/diligence

Yardley, S. (2015, March 30). Retrieved from Cross Doorway Clipart: http://www.christart.com/clipart/image/open-door-cross

Yardley, S., & Peruchini, L. (2015, March 30). *Christart.com/clipart/image/open-door-cross.* Retrieved from Golden Cros Doorway Clipart: http://www.christart.com/clipart/image/open-door-cross

# NOTES

www.ingramcontent.com/pod-product-compliance
Lightning Source LLC
LaVergne TN
LVHW051504070426
835507LV00022B/2916